For Virginia Business Owners In Manufacturing and Service Industries In The Growth Zone of $1M - $25M revenue

The

GROWTH ZONE

10 Roadblocks You Must Overcome To Create a Business with Enduring Value

MICHAEL MITCHELL

Virginia's #1 Trusted Authority On Growing Enduring Business Value

outskirts
press

Table of Contents

Introduction

You are probably reading this book because you are the owner of a manufacturing or service business and you want to grow your business. You and your business have had a roller coaster ride as you have been challenged by competition that was bigger and better funded than you. You have been challenged by employees you were sure would be a great fit, only to let them go a few months later. Financial struggles were always on your mind in the early days, and they are never off your mind for long now. You have introduced new products and services in order to grow and some were well received, while others were met with a mediocre response. Your growth has slowed to the point that you feel like you are treading water, expending a great deal of energy just to keep your head above the waterline. Now your overhead is starting to worry you. You have good years and some not so good years. But you never stop trying.

The Growth Zone

Despite the many challenges you have faced, you still made it into what I call "The Growth Zone", which is the $1M - $25M revenue range. But the Growth Zone also has many pitfalls that must be avoided and roadblocks that need to be swatted aside. I have known many business owners who made into the Growth Zone, only to fall out a short time later. Others grow into the Growth Zone, and then quickly plateau. When that happens, you can feel like Sisyphus pushing his stone up the mountain. And every day is the same long climb.

This book is about growing a business with enduring value once you are in the Growth Zone. Growing means growing your revenue, growing your earnings, growing your employees, putting in the appropriate infrastructure, and generally becoming a more sophisticated business that can compete with the industry leaders in your market.

The Ignition Zone

I have organized this book into three sections which follow the natural growth of a business. Not every business will grapple with the three roadblocks outlined in the Ignition Zone ($1M to $5M), but most will. Not every business will deal with these roadblocks effectively. However, clearing these roadblocks is fundamental to growth. While in the ignition Zone you lay the foundation that allows future growth to occur in a smooth and organized fashion. Think of this zone as igniting the main engines of your business. If the engines are not running properly, you will not achieve Lift-Off. You will be stuck on the ground and may fall out of the Growth Zone altogether.

The Lift-Off Zone

When you first enter the Lift-Off Zone ($5M to $15M) any lingering roadblocks from the Ignition Zone should be dispatched quickly, or they will cause major problems as your business continues to grow. Your business is now flying somewhere quickly, so you better be sure you know where that is, and how to get there because there are 4 big roadblocks on your horizon. These roadblocks will stop your business in its tracks and you will be pushed to the limits of your knowledge and capability to remove them. But deal with them effectively and you will build a business with enduring value. Your business will become a powerhouse in your chosen market and your reputation in the business community will grow along with your business. When you decide to exit your business, you will have options and you will be able to achieve all your exit goals. Navigate this zone adeptly and you will be ready to fire your booster rockets and enter the Acceleration Zone ($15 to $25M).

The Acceleration Zone

The Acceleration Zone is currently entered into by only a small fraction of all businesses. But that needn't be the case. If you have knocked aside the roadblocks leading up to the Acceleration Zone, you are ready to clear away the final few obstacles that can keep you in the Growth Zone. Once those are cleared away, you can grow your business into a regional or national powerhouse. Your business will be limited only by your own ambitions.

The Map

This book is about growing a business with enduring value once you are in the Growth Zone. Growing means growing your revenue, growing your earnings, growing your employees, growing your leadership skills, putting in the appropriate infrastructure, and generally becoming a more sophisticated business that can compete with the industry leaders in your market. It also means doing all these things in a way that grows your capability so that your business becomes more valuable to you. Greater value means you will have more and better options when you are ready to leave your business.

Think of this book as a roadmap. The map is not the territory, and the territory as you encounter it will probably be different from the map. The key is to understand the concepts introduced in each section and apply them to your unique situation. Building a business and navigating the roadmap does not need to be a solitary heroic adventure. There are resources available to help you as you follow the path I have laid out. Reach out to these resources and learn from them. You do not need to make the same mistakes your coaches and mentors have made, you only need to make your own mistakes.

Do you want to be average, or do you want to be the leader in your industry? What stops you from dominating your market space? What determines your margins? What limits your growth? The short answer to all of these questions is your perspective. So, would you be open to new ways of thinking about the roadblocks that prevent you from growing, and how to swat those roadblocks aside? Or, is average good enough?

I am guessing that average is never good enough for you and that you will keep reading. If your ultimate goal is to be able to leave your business when you want, for the money you want, and transfer it to the successor of your choosing, then you must create enduring value. Let me show you how.

If this book resonates with you and you can relate to any of the roadblocks discussed in the chapters you're about to read, then book a Complimentary no charge Growth Strategy Consultation (value $995.00) by going to https://brgbrokers.com/freeconsult

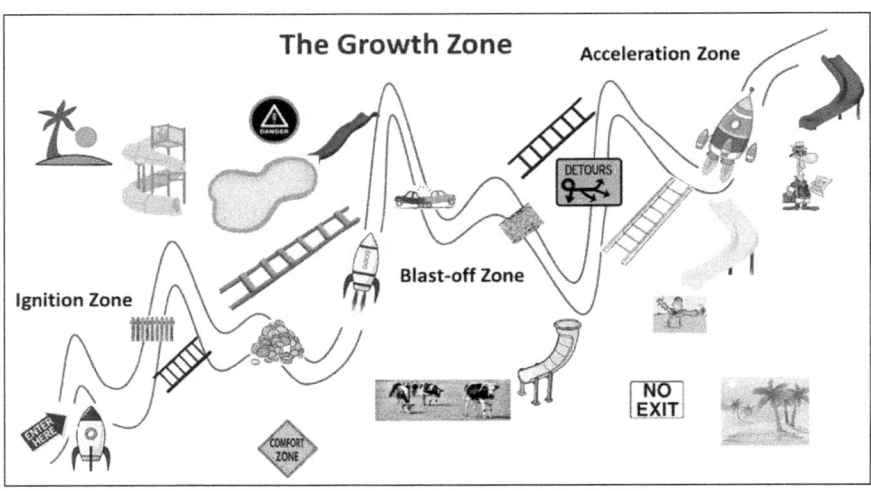

My Story

I am currently enjoying my 4th career and running 4 businesses. Over the past 15 years, my company The Valuation Authority has valued hundreds of small businesses, and for most business owners the news was very disappointing. I started Growth Zone University, LLC to help owners close the gap between the business' real value and what she was hoping it was worth. Once the value gap has been closed and the owner can exit her business for the price she needs, Business Research Group, LLC, my M&A business, finds buyers and closes the deal.

We are the only firm in Virginia focused on small businesses, that also has all three of these critical services in-house. If you want to eventually sell your business for more than $1M you need to know what it is worth today, you need to create enduring value, and you need to find the buyer willing to pay you the most money. That is what we do.

I received bachelor degrees in Chemistry and Chemical Engineering from Penn State and stayed on to get my Master's degree in Chemical Engineering. Armed with a lot of knowledge about product and process, I started my first career in big business, designing and producing new products and the associated new manufacturing processes. That career culminated when I was managing a global new product and new business development organization. While I enjoyed that career, my desire to learn more about business kept nagging at me so I went back to school and earned my MBA from Virginia Commonwealth University.

Soon thereafter I began my second career in sales, marketing, and big business management. After a while the corporate politics and the merry-go-round of "high flying" managers around me made me feel like I was stuck in a bad dream. Then one day it hit me. Quit. Do something else. Open a lemonade stand if you have to, but do something else. So, I did.

I started my third career as an entrepreneur importing industrial products. In 5 years, I was able to ramp up that business in a way that it attracted the attention of a much larger competitor. I was enjoying running my business, but when the opportunity came along, I decided to cash out and sold to the larger corporation. I built that business in a way that created enduring value, and as a result, I achieved all my goals when I exited that business. I sold it for the amount I needed, I exited when I was ready, and I sold to a buyer who could continue to grow and build the business.

Now, in my fourth career, I coach other business owners to grow their business. Not just their revenue and earnings, but to grow enduring value as well.

Outskirts Press, Inc.
http://www.outskirtspress.com

ISBN: 978-1-9772-1754-7

Outskirts Press and the "OP" logo are trademarks belonging to Outskirts Press, Inc.

PRINTED IN THE UNITED STATES OF AMERICA

The Ignition Zone
$1M to $5M of revenue

CHAPTER 1

Time (Self) Management

Roadblock #1: I have to get an order out by Friday, I can't waste my time sitting in a conference room talking about growth.

> "Things which matter most must never be at the
> mercy of things which matter least."
> - Johann Wolfgang von Goethe

IF YOU ARE in the Growth Zone, you are probably proud of your business and how you have grown it from nothing to over $1M in revenue, and you should be proud of that accomplishment. Very few businesses sustain revenue of more than $1M. It is at this point that you have a choice to make. You can continue to run your business the way you have been doing for the past 5, 10, or 20 years. Or, you can make the changes needed to grow enduring value.

Change your Perception

I have heard all the reasons, justifications, and excuses for not growing a business. Some owners lack the motivation to pursue growth and enduring value. They reason that they are doing pretty well now, so why add all that work and hassle to their plate? Other owners do not see how to grow in their industry, and without a clear plan to grow, growth is left to chance. Some have partners who cannot agree on the best path to follow. Others feel that they don't have the resources to grow their business, and some are so consumed by the urgent demands of the day that growth never makes it to the top of the To-Do list.

When you're busy managing your company's day-to-day operations, you can feel as though you simply don't have time to do anything else. When the phone rings, you answer it. When employees have questions, you answer them. When production has a problem, you are out on the floor gathering information and finding the root cause. You have meetings to preside over, luncheons to attend, and phone calls to return. Everyone wants a piece of your time, and you give it to them because nobody knows your business the way you do. Already stretched to the limit, you have little time for thinking seriously about growing your business.

Work on the Right Things

If you do not have time to grow and create value, I suggest that while you are busy and working a lot of hours, you are working on the wrong things. The process of growing enduring value involves changing your perception of your role in the business. When you reimagine your role in your business, you will end up with more time, more freedom, and more money. The process begins with goal setting and doesn't end until you finally walk away from your business.

Challenge Yourself

I challenge you to set a goal of growing your business to the point that you can be an absentee owner. You may not want to ever be an absentee owner, but having the ability to do so requires you to think about your business and your role in ways that you never imagined possible.

There are strategies you can use to turn over some responsibility and authority to key employees which will ultimately give you more control over your business and your life. Transforming yourself from the hub of your company to the coach of the team is a challenge that many business owners fail to overcome. In the process, they sabotage their efforts at a successful business exit down the road.

You may find it difficult to break the habits you have trained yourself, your customers, and your employees, to follow. But let me be clear, you can no longer be the fixer of all problems, the fountain of all information, and the maker of all decisions. When you remove yourself from these roles, you will find that 30% or more of your time is freed up for the more important work of growing enduring value.

Recognize Opportunities

I know, that order still has to go out by Friday, and you are the one who can make that happen, so you take the time to solve whatever problems are keeping the order from shipping on time. I get it. But you should also see that there are opportunities in this situation. An opportunity to create a process that prevents a crisis from happening in the first place. An opportunity to train employees on how to handle the situation in the future. An opportunity to delight a customer be-cause they never receive a phone call on Friday afternoon alerting them that their order did not ship so they will not receive it on time. You need to free up the time to work on these more strategic oppor-tunities. And there is an easy way to do that.

Opportunities for staff to grow

As you start to remove yourself from some activities, you may no-tice that there are opportunities to rearrange the workflow and assign-ments in your office. Your current office staff may be able to take over the administrative functions you don't enjoy by changing their roles and assignments. Increased productivity is often achieved when the employees are given a voice in the process of organizing and defining their roles. There may be no need to hire anyone new, and there may be an opportunity to reward those employees for helping you make the transition. If you don't have one already, a good office manager can handle many of the tasks you will want to delegate and make the office run much more smoothly.

Reduce Turnover

If your business is not growing, you probably do not have the cash to give employees raises and they do not have opportunities for promotions. You probably find that some employees join your company, grow out of their job, and leave to take a job with another company that can meet their financial, psychological, and intellectual needs. It costs you money to recruit, hire, and train employees. And it may take 6 months to a year before new employees are fully contributing members of your team so employee turnover costs you a great deal of money.

You want to retain top employees, and pay is a big part of every plan. In fact, fair pay is one of the five keys to retention. Fair pay means paying fairly compared to the market value for the job, fairly based on stated organizational values and priorities, and fairly based on the employee's performance and results. But money is only one means to retain key employees.

Employees want their opinions to count, and they don't want to be ignored. A full-time employee generally spends more waking hours on the job than at home, and she wants that time to be meaningful. Employees value the freedom to complete their assignments in a way that feels most comfortable for them. Managers who insist that "it's my way or the highway" frustrate employees and cause them to begin considering other employment options. By giving key employees more authority to plan, schedule, and implement key objectives they grow in their capabilities and experience, and they become more valuable.

Organizations that offer the ability to do meaningful work are finding an edge over their competition. Managing turnover is about mindfully creating a workplace culture that supports high performers financially, intellectually, and psychologically while at the same time providing a means to efficiently and fairly weed out poor performers who compromise company goals and values. Retaining your top talent means getting to know your employees and what matters to them individually. In my experience, when employees are given the opportunity and authority to organize and plan their work they will rise to the task.

Develop High-Performance Habits

High performance is not achieved by a specific kind of person, but rather by a specific set of practices. High performing people, whether they are world-class athletes, CEOs of large corporations, coaches, celebrities, or business owners in the Growth Zone, have learned that to reach and sustain high levels of performance you have to develop the habits of high performance.

Developing these deliberate habits won't come easily. You have to practice them with real mental focus. Every time you feel stuck, every time you start a new project, every time you measure your progress, every time you lead others, you must deliberately think about the high-performance habits. You'll have to use them as a checklist, just as a pilot uses a preflight checklist before every takeoff.

High productivity starts with goals. Once you have clarity about what you want to achieve, you can begin to develop the habit of focusing on what is important, choosing how you spend the time you are given each day and delegating the less important tasks to others on your team.

Manage Yourself

Managing a growing business begins with managing yourself, and what you choose to accomplish every day. Many consultants call it time management, but we all are given exactly the same amount of time every day. We can't slow it down, borrow from tomorrow, or manage it in any way. No one starts the day with more time than you have. It's what you do with that time that counts. It's how you manage yourself that counts.

If you have well-defined goals, you can start every day with the knowledge of what you must accomplish that day with the time you have. Focus on activities that will bring you closer to achieving your goals. Those activities are important and you should schedule a time to work on them.

You will also be tempted to work on a variety of activities that appear to be urgent. But most activities that are urgent are not important. Use the chart below to help you decide what to work on every day.

	NOT URGENT	URGENT
IMPORTANT	**Quadrant 2** Important But Not Urgent *Relationships* *Strategic Planning* *New Opportunities*	**Quadrant 1** Important And Urgent Crises *Deadlines* *Problems*
NOT IMPORTANT	**Quadrant 4** Not Important, Not Urgent *Time Wasters* *Pleasant Activities* *Trivia* *Busywork*	**Quadrant 3** Not Important, But Urgent *Interruptions* *Some Meetings* *Some Phone calls* *Distractions*

If you want to grow your business, your challenge as a business owner is to reduce the amount of time you spend in Quadrants 3 and 4 and increase the time you spend in Quadrants 1 and 2.

Getting an important order shipped to an important customer may be a Q1 activity, and you should give it your highest priority. A related Q2 activity is designing a scheduling and fulfillment process and then training your employees how to follow the process so that shipping the order on time happens without any involvement from you.

When presented with an opportunity to spend your time on any activity, you must ask two questions:

- Is this activity crucial to me achieving my goals?
- Is this activity on the critical path for me to achieve my goals?

The critical path goes through those projects that when completed in the proper sequence add up to the longest overall duration. The critical path determines the shortest time possible to achieve your goal. If an activity is on the critical path, it is by definition an urgent project.

If you answer yes to both questions, it means the activity is both important and urgent and therefore a Q1 activity. Q1 activities deserve your time and attention with high priority. If you answer yes to only the first question, then you probably have a Q2 activity, important and worthy of your time, but if there are Q1 activities you can work on, you should complete those first.

If the answer to the first question is no, then you have a Q3 or Q4 activity. Quadrant 4 is where we go to zone out and stare at the television, play a video game, or get sucked into the vortex of social media. Sometimes we want some Q4 activities to relax and wind down after a particularly trying day. The occasional Q4 activity is fine. Think of it as the occasional treat you might give yourself while watching your diet. But, you cannot let it become a habit that consumes your Q1/Q2 activity time.

Q3 activities are all around us. They press on us and they insist on action. They are often hot button items championed by others. They're usually right in front of us and often they are pleasant, easy, and fun to do. But they are unimportant!

Q3 activities are like cosmic quicksand. They will suck your time into a black hole and will consume all of it if you allow it. You get sucked in because these activities appear to be urgent; they have deadlines and appear to be important. But when you dig deeper, you realize that the urgency is from the perspective of the person who wants to involve you, and the activity does not help you accomplish your goals.

The key to avoiding this quicksand is to ask the first of the above two questions again. If you are not sure if this activity will help you achieve your goals, it may be that you need to have better clarity around your goals. But if the answer is no, you have a Q3 activity and beware that black holes have an infinite capacity to consume time.

How Buyers Perceive Value

For most owners cashing out of your business means selling to a third-party. Every buyer wants to hear that the business they are considering has great potential. Indeed, they are unlikely to buy your business if it does not have potential. But, make no mistake, they will not pay you for potential. Potential is the reward they earn when they take on the risk of achieving that potential with their hard work, initiative, and persistence. They will pay you for what you have already demonstrated, but even then, they must believe that the financial returns you demonstrated the past few years are highly likely to continue into the future after you are gone. Without that confidence, the price they will be willing to pay for your business will be highly discounted.

Reduce Your Value to Increase Business Value

There is an inverse relationship between your importance to the business and its value. The more valuable you are to your business, the less valuable your business is to you. Since enduring value is what buyers pay for, every growth strategy you undertake should be designed in a way that your business can operate well without you.

Make Building Value Urgent

If you do not perceive the strategic work of growing value as urgent, it won't happen. You will postpone it to next week, which becomes next month, and then next year. And then one day you find 10 years have got behind you. No one told you when to run, you missed the starting gun. (My apologies to David Gilmour.) So, you tell a potential buyer that "This business has tremendous potential!" What you don't add is "All you have to do, is all the things I was unable or unwilling to do."

Start sooner for better results

When business owners start to seriously consider exiting their business, the most common regret they express is not starting the process of growing value sooner. In almost all situations, starting early provides you with more options, more control, and a better chance of achieving all your exit goals. It can take you 2 to 7 years to fully implement the actions needed to grow enduring value. With that much lead time, doesn't it make sense to start growing a valuable business today?

Jim's Story

Jim had worked a variety of construction jobs as an apprentice in his father's handyman business during summers while he was in high school, and throughout the year while he was attending college. After graduating with a degree in business, Jim started his own design/build firm. He quickly became known for the high quality of his work and enjoyed the patronage of a number of influential families throughout the local area. He won several prestigious awards for his designs.

After 7 years, Jim had grown his home renovation business to $3 million in revenue. His total compensation and other distributions totaled $240,000, which provided his family with all of their needs and most of their wants. Jim had been handling almost every aspect of the business and was overwhelmed. He met with potential clients, did most of the design work, stopped in on ongoing projects to oversee installation, and at nights did payroll and accounting. He rarely saw his family, and when he did, he was constantly checking his phone.

His business had plateaued 2 years earlier. The economy, interest rates, the Fed, and government regulations all conspired to prevent him from growing any further. He needed another estimator, but all the good ones were taken. Another salesperson was needed to bring in more business, but he had already gone through 3 "experienced" salespeople in the past 6 months. They either quit or were shown the door.

We worked through several goal-setting exercises and for the first time since Jim started his company, he could articulate a vision of where he wanted to take his business. Jim saw how delegating many of his current responsibilities to others within the company would give him back some of his lost family time, without jeopardizing his control of the company. This eventually allowed Jim to reduce his workweek to between 30 and 40 hours. He is still the company's deal closer and maintains many of the most important customer relationships, but he has delegated many less critical and less enjoyable tasks to others. He now spends most of his time with Q2 and some Q3 activities. While the work he does is less hands-on, he is still deeply involved in financial and key business decisions.

Jim chose to use his free time by joining the boards of 2 nonprofits he wanted to support, and he now attends almost all of his children's little league games and soccer matches.

The Bank

There is a story about a bank that credits your account each morning with $86,400. It carries over no balance from one day to the next. Every evening the bank deletes whatever part of the balance you failed to spend during the day. If you fail to use the day's deposits, the loss is yours.

Each of us has such a bank and its name is TIME. Every morning, it credits you with 86,400 seconds. It carries over no balance. It allows no overdraft. There is no going back. There is no drawing against tomorrow. Every day you must live in the present on today's deposit.

Invest this deposit wisely and the return on your investment will be health, happiness, and success. The clock is running. Make the most of today. Yesterday is history. Tomorrow is a mystery. Today is a gift. That's why it's called the present!

Key take-aways

The first inflection point that causes many business owners to change their perception of their business and their role in the business comes when they no longer have the time to do everything well, and as a result, their business growth slows considerably. The business plateaus and they do not know how to break through that slump.

Long before the time comes when you, as the manager owner can no longer effectively manage your business, you must start learning how to work with employees and colleagues, learn how to trust those you have hired, and learn how to give them the authority and responsibility to make decisions while still holding them accountable.

You must learn to become the leader of a team rather than a star with helpers. You can learn to prioritize, delegate, eliminate, and schedule. By doing this you can save 20 hours per week that you can use for leisure time, or to work on the strategic issues of growing your business with enduring value.

CHAPTER 2

Strategy and Goals

Roadblock #2: I finally have the business in a good stable place, why do I need to change it?

> "The tragedy of life is often not in our failure, but rather in our complacency; not in our doing too much, but rather in our doing too little; not in our living above our ability, but rather in our living below our capacities." –Benjamin E. Mays

Acceptance of the status quo

IT'S ALMOST INEVITABLE. When you first started out, you did whatever was necessary to make your business successful. You dreamed of the day when you hit X number of customers or $X in revenue or earnings. You worked hard to achieve success. You've struggled through hard times, you've met challenges head-on, and you've won the hard battles. You've finally reached a level of success of which you are justifiably proud.

You are in the Growth Zone and you are enjoying a personal income level that few business owners achieve. You drive a new car, take expensive vacations, you have an awesome home entertainment system, and perhaps a country club membership along with the expectation of having the free time to enjoy it all.

As you relax and enjoy your success, you take your foot off the business gas pedal and slow down a bit. You tell yourself it is just for a short time. You tell yourself that you will get back to growing your business after this well-deserved break.

Without the pressure to achieve new goals, you are likely to lose motivation and lose your focus. The short time that you planned to take off will stretch into a month, then a year. You have now entered the "Comfort Zone."

There is nothing wrong with being in the Comfort Zone. But Beware, it is not easy to remain there. You can drop out at any time, and it may not be on your terms. While achieving success was hard, staying successful is even harder and you're about to face your toughest challenge yet. If you are in the Comfort Zone, you are vulnerable to falling into a Complacency Trap.

The Complacency Trap

Complacency is a business killer. It can strike anytime, anywhere, at any level. Owner, CEO, manager, supervisor, marketing department, production line, and delivery drivers, are all vulnerable. A Complacency Trap is like quicksand. It sucks you in slowly, and by the time you realize what has happened, it may be too late for you to escape on your own.

Your employees take their cues from you. They see you behaving differently. They know you no longer have a fire in your belly, and they begin to relax as well. Complacency starts with you but quickly spreads like the measles to infect your entire business.

Once employees are infected, customers will notice the change. Excellence is replaced by good, and soon thereafter with "good enough." Service will begin to slip, orders will ship late, and AR will stretch out to 60 or 90 days. Without new goals to achieve, employees become bored, they don't work as hard, and the likelihood of you perpetuating your success is greatly reduced.

When growth is left to chance, your chances are awfully good there will be no growth

In my experience, if you are in a Complacency Trap you will never take the first step towards setting and achieving new goals. Your business will stop growing because, without new goals, there is no motivation to do any better. You will begin to believe that the lack of growth is due to the Fed, the economy, tariffs, regulations or competitors. You will never point the finger of guilt at the mirror.

When you are in a Complacency Trap, you may speak passionately about how difficult it is to run your business, but you have taken no steps to make a change. Perhaps, you may not know what to change, or how to change it. And you may be reluctant to ask for help.

Admitting that you need help in order to continue to grow your business can be a blow to your ego. You want to break out of the trap you are in, but the cure of setting goals, developing plans to achieve your goals, and managing for achievement all seem more painful than the lack of growth. So, you convince yourself that nothing can be done to change your situation.

Thinking Strategically leads to Growth

You have reached the second inflection point in your journey to grow enduring value. I challenge you to avoid the Comfort Zone. Do not accept the status quo. Keep Growing! Not just growing your revenue, but growing your profitability, your capability, and enduring value.

Prior to entering the Growth Zone, you may have gotten by without thinking about strategy, setting goals, or planning to achieve those goals. Maybe you thought about these ideas but kept them in your head where no one but you knew they existed. If you want to grow enduring value that has to change now. You must look at everything you are doing systematically to be certain that you have the best chance possible of creating enduring value.

Competitive strategy is not a "Game of Thrones" sequel. A strategy is the direction and scope of an organization over the long term which achieves competitive advantage through its deployment of re-sources and competencies. It is not about doing things better than your competition, it is about being different from your competition. It means deliberately choosing a different set of activities to deliver a unique mix of value.

Porter on Strategy

Your company can outperform the competition only if it can es-tablish a difference that it can preserve. Michael Porter in his 1980 book *Competitive Strategy* identified 3 generic strategies for outper-forming your competition in any industry: low-cost production, prod-uct innovation and differentiation, and customer focus.

The first strategy is to achieve overall cost leadership in any indus-try through a set of functional policies aimed at this basic objective. Cost leadership requires aggressive construction of efficient-scale fa-cilities, vigorous pursuit of cost reductions from experience, tight cost and overhead control, avoidance of marginal customer accounts, and cost minimization in areas like R&D, service, salesforce, advertising, and so on. A great deal of managerial attention to cost control is necessary to achieve these aims. Low cost relative to competitors be-comes the theme running through the entire strategy, though quality, service, and other areas cannot be ignored.

The second generic strategy is one of differentiating the product or service offering of your business, creating something that is per-ceived industry-wide as being unique. Approaches to differentiation can take many forms: design or brand image (Fieldcrest in top of the line towels and linens; Mercedes in automobiles), technology (Hyster in lift trucks; McIntosh in stereo components; Coleman in camping equipment), features (Jenn-Air in electric ranges); customer service (Crown Cork and Seal in metal cans), dealer network (Caterpillar Tractor in construction equipment), or other dimensions. Ideally, your business differentiates itself along several dimensions. Caterpillar Tractor, for example, is known not only for its dealer network and ex-cellent spare parts availability but also for its extremely high-quality durable products, all of which are crucial in heavy equipment where downtime is very expensive. It should be stressed that the differentiation strategy does not allow your business to ignore costs, but rather they are not the primary strategic target.

The final generic strategy is focusing on a particular buyer group, a segment of the product line, or geographic market. A focus strategy may take many forms. Although the low cost and differentiation strategies are aimed at achieving their objectives industrywide, the entire focus strategy is built around serving a particular target very well, and each functional policy is developed with this in mind. The strategy rests on the premise that the firm is able to serve its narrow strategic target more effectively or efficiently than competitors who are competing more broadly. As a result, your business achieves either differentiation from better meeting the needs of the particular target, or lower costs in serving this target, or both. Even though the focus strategy does not achieve low cost or differentiation from the perspective of the market as a whole, it does achieve one or both of these positions within its narrow target market.

Ultimately, all differences between companies in cost or price derive from the hundreds of activities required to create, produce, sell, and deliver their products or services, such as calling on customers, assembling final products, and training employees. Cost is generated by performing activities, and cost advantage arises from performing particular activities more efficiently than competitors. Similarly, differentiation arises from both the choice of activities and how they are performed. Activities, then, are the basic units of competitive advantage. Overall advantage or disadvantage results from all a company's activities, not only a few.

To succeed in business, no matter what business you are in, you are going to need a great strategy. You don't have to be the only business in your market in order to succeed. You don't need to have the best product or service in the world in order to win. You need to be the best at serving your ideal customers. Success in business is actually as much about strategy as it is about the actual product that is being sold. Of course, it helps to have a great product, but you need an excellent strategy to match.

For far too many leaders, developing a strategy is a struggle. Despite all the different tools available (or perhaps because of them), developing a strategy can seem mysterious and scary. That needn't be the case. Strategy can be defined and created using a simple framework that entails answering five questions — the same five questions, no matter the type, size or context of the organization.

Lafley and Martin's Five-Step Strategy Model is built on five integrated questions.

- What should be the winning aspiration?
- Where you are going to play?
- How you are going to win?
- What capabilities should you build?
- What management systems are needed?

Answering the above questions requires a deep knowledge of your business as well as what is going on in the market.

What Is Your Winning Aspiration?

Quite simply, this is the goal of the organization. Of course, it should be a bit more specific than just stating that you would like to make money. All for-profit businesses want to make money, so that doesn't really help you get anywhere. To make it more specific think about:

- What it is that you are going to do in order to make that money?
- Are you trying to dominate a specific market?
- Do you want to capture a small piece of a big market?

It is important to be specific even at this top-level, as your answers to this question will influence decisions you make later on. The best way to think about this question is to picture what success would look like in the future. If your organization is successful five years from now, what would that look like? You should be optimistic, but realistic at the same time. For instance, if you sell some form of technology, you likely aren't going to topple the major players in the tech game, but that doesn't mean you can't be successful.

Where Will You Compete?

Once you know what it will look like to win, you then need to decide exactly where you are going to compete in order to achieve that victory. This question demands that you identify both the markets and the customers that you are going to pursue.

For some businesses, such as those that sell directly to consumers, the answers to this question will be easy. For example, if you produce a small product that is easy to ship, and you are selling directly to consumers, you will probably set up a website in addition to selling on other established e-commerce sites.

However, for businesses that are going to sell to distributors or other intermediaries, identifying specific markets and channels may take a bit more time and effort.

How Will You Win?

Now that you know where you are going to be competing in the market, the next step to deal with is the strategy that you are going to use to make sure you come out on top.

You are going to face competition in whatever slice of the market you have decided to enter, so you will need to think long and hard about how you can position your product or service to stand out from the rest. If you take this step for granted, you will probably find that your competition remains a step ahead of you for years to come.

You don't need to have a complex strategy in place at this level to come out on top but it does need to be a good strategy that has a real chance to succeed. You could plan on winning the market based on lower cost, higher quality, faster turnaround times, better customer service, or some combination of those three.

What Capabilities Must We Have in Place to Win?

This is the infrastructure that supports the plans you have developed. In order to enter the selected markets, and win in those markets, you will need a specific set of capabilities in place within your organization. What are you going to need to do in order to meet your goals?

For instance, if you have decided that you are going to win by offering lower prices, what capabilities to do you need to be able to sell your goods at a low price point? What are your core competencies (activities that you are good at) that are going to enable you to win?

What management systems and measures are going to help me execute?

The last of the five essential questions is about management systems, the systems that build, support and measure the success of your chosen strategy. This last question is typically the most neglected but is no less crucial to effective strategy than the others. Even if the other four questions are well answered, a strategy will fail if management systems that support the choices and capabilities are not established as well.

Without supporting structures, systems, and measures, the strategy will simply be a wishlist, a set of goals that will never be achieved. You need a robust process for creating, reviewing, and communicating your strategy. You need structures to support its core capabilities and you need specific measures to determine whether the strategy is working or not. You need to decide who you need, how to enable them, and how you can tell whether the strategy is succeeding.

Companies with enduring value select a strategy and stick with it, enhancing it over time. They incorporate these strategies into their talent management processes: who they hire, how they manage people, who they promote, and how people grow in the organization. You must staff, manage, and incentivize people consistent with your chosen strategy. The goals you determine will support the strategy you have chosen.

Staff Meetings

If you have grown your business to the point that you have managers in place for sales, operations, customer service, and other functional areas, you have the team that can help you identify the best strategy for your business, and you have an opportunity to focus that team on growth.

If you have staff meetings, they are probably focused on the burning operational issues of the day, or on reviewing operational dashboards with little discussions of the 3rd, 4th or 5th "why" for what's behind your average or lackluster performance. Here are five questions that you may wish to discuss with your staff. If you do not yet have a team, you should be asking yourself these questions.

1. Why are we losing business? (Have participants write down their top three reasons, then share). Hint, if your price is in the top 3 answers it is time to shake things up.

2. Who is our ideal customer? What makes them ideal? Who are our most profitable customers? What do they have in common? Are there more of them? Are they delighted with us? What other problems do they have that we could solve?

3. Are any of our value propositions interchangeable with our competitors? If so, what is our unique value and how do we clearly communicate that message? What sets us apart?

4. Should we be offering more, or less, choice in our product portfolio? Why? How would our demand and cost curves change if we eliminated the bottom 20% of our offering? Is there a clear owner of SKU count and range rationalization? Is there a clear champion for finding new applications for our existing products?

5. What potential sales partnerships and industry alliances

should we be planning for in our future? Are there channel partners that could take us to adjacent markets? Are there technology partners that could help us expand our range without a significant engineering investment? Is there a complimentary party that would allow us efficient entry into an international market? Are there opportunities with an emerging technology partner that will allow us to gain both insights and an early market presence?

Growth focused companies outperform operationally focused companies. Asking these questions at your staff meetings has the potential to accelerate your growth and make your meetings more engaging.

Bob's Story

I have worked with many entrepreneurs who have reimagined their business model as an organized, effective system that emphasizes process as a way to grow their business. Every part of their business was systematically examined in order to ensure that the process could be duplicated in another office utilizing a team of trained personnel. I have also met many business owners like Bob.

Bob's story represents the stories of so many business owners I have met over the years. They were hardworking, honest, and good people. Things did not work out as well as they could have, but they never complained. They kept on doing what they thought was best. And they remained unaware of all the possibilities they were missing.

The Entrepreneurial Seizure

Bob worked for a large cable manufacturer. The cables were used in a variety of industrial, and defense equipment, and some consumer applications. Bob had an engineering background and always found ways to improve the current manufacturing process. He was constantly improving it. Unfortunately, his bosses constantly told Bob why he could not make any changes to the current process. Bob was feeling underappreciated and overworked when he was hit by an entrepreneurial seizure.

He decided he would start his own business, design his own processes, design the products, and do it all faster and cheaper than his old company. He would also get all the reward. He wisely chose to focus his business, Virginia Cables on a very particular niche, one that was too small for the big companies to bother with and required a level of technical expertise that most of the small companies did not possess.

Bob Enters the Growth Zone

Bob quickly grew his revenue and earnings. He was now in the Growth Zone, and with just shy of $4M in revenue, he was earning just over $200K in total compensation. His wife Tina worked in the business keeping the books a few days each week, while Bob oversaw design, operations, most of the sales, and they shared the financial responsibility.

Bob worked 60 hours a week. He made sales calls, approved payments, did some design work, responded to bid requests, and expedited orders when the plant was running behind, which seemed to happen regularly lately. He could not understand how production could get behind now since revenue had dipped slightly the past year.

Bob had always been a hands-on manager, and he was proud of the fact that he was the hub that kept the business wheel turning. Whenever employees had questions about how to complete a job, Bob was the fountain of all information. When a decision had to be made about customer service issues, Bob decided how the issue should be handled. When orders were in jeopardy of shipping late Bob was out there on the factory floor checking gauges and making certain that the machines were set up correctly, the equipment was working properly, and doing whatever was necessary to get the order out.

As Tina and Bob both approached turning 58, Tina began to bring up the subject of retirement more frequently. She also began to talk about vacations they had put off, places she wanted to visit, and experiences she wanted to have while they were still in great health. Trains, planes, cruise ships, and automobiles were all featured in her ongoing commentary. After all, she reasoned, we have saved a lot of money; the business is bringing in plenty of money, and they could simply hire a manager to run the business, pay him $100K, and they can keep the rest. They could finally enjoy the fruit of all their hard work.

One day Tina made it clear that she was not going to work past age 60. She was planning to take a long vacation after her retirement and Bob was invited and encouraged to come along with her, but if he would rather work, she was going alone.

As Tina continued to talk about "their plan" to retire at 60, Bob began to see the logic in this narrative. The business had stopped growing. Some years had a small year over year growth in revenue, but then they would have a bust year that put them back to where they were 3 years earlier. Margins had fallen some, but that was because of increased competition, and the low end of their business had been taken by overseas competitors. There was nothing he could do about that. Things were tough, and Bob no longer had a passion to grow the business. He had entered the Comfort Zone. He agreed with Tina that they should hire a manager and he could act as the CEO in hiding.

Bob chooses a Successor

Bob advertised for the plant manager position and received a number of responses. As he interviewed potential candidates, he realized that none of them had his experience in the industry, they all wanted far too much money, and none seemed to be a good fit with his style of management. He wanted someone who could do things the way he had always done them. They just needed to be younger, have more energy, and bring new ideas. He decided that the best thing to do was to promote his best technician, Allen, who had been with the company for almost 15 years.

Allen was a hard worker and knew how to set up the machines and how to tweak them to get the best results. He welcomed the opportunity to take on the new role as plant manager. Bob and Tina would continue to control the checkbook, and oversee the finances of the business, but Allen would make sure the orders were processed, built, and shipped on time. Allen also had the responsibility of growing sales.

While Allen had no experience in sales, he reasoned that he could learn how to do sales. After all, Bob had no formal sales training and he grew the business to $4M in revenue. Selling was just getting to know the customer and keeping them happy by supplying them with what they wanted. Anybody could learn that.

Bob and Allen struck a deal and spent the next month together, meeting customers, talking with suppliers, learning how to handle payroll, customer service issues, payables, receivables, design standards, and all the details of managing the business Allen never knew existed. Allen drank from the fountain of all information for a month and then took over as the Virginia Cables plant manager.

While on a 2-week cruise from Paris to Avignon Bob admitted to Tina that life in the Comfort Zone was indeed very enjoyable. He was glad that Tina had persisted in her efforts to coax him into the Zone, and they were finally able to spend some money they had saved.

Remove the Hub and the Wheel Collapses

Unbeknownst to Bob, his business began to suffer from his absence almost immediately. While Allen was a great technician, he did not have the knowledge that Bob possessed. When employees asked Allen questions about jobs, he often did not know how to answer them. He told the employees to figure it out the best they could. After all, that was how Allen learned. That response was frustrating for the employees who wanted to do a good job and frustrating to Allen who wished he had better answers for them.

A few months after Allen took over, he received a fairly large order from a new customer. If they did a good job on this order, it was an opportunity to gain a good chunk of ongoing new business. Since growth was part of Allen's responsibility, he was delighted to get the order. It was a technically demanding order, and they did not have the equipment to do the job in the most efficient way. The equipment was expensive, and Allen was not authorized to buy new equipment. He decided that he could make some minor modifications to the existing equipment that would allow them to run the order. The job would run more slowly than their regular process, but they could run it on the modified equipment and ship on time. Allen did his happy dance.

The equipment modifications took the machine shop longer than expected, and once Allen started it up, he realized they would need to do some tweaking to meet the specs for the job. After a few more days of dialing in the equipment, they were ready to begin running the job. By this time, they were already behind schedule. As expected, the machine ran slower than their normal process, so to catch up Allen authorized overtime and everyone worked double shifts to complete the job. Allen authorized expedited shipping to get the order to the customer a few days earlier. Allen was delighted that they were able to ship the order to the customer and that it would only be 2 weeks later than promised. When Allen thought about it a year later, he realized he never heard back from that customer.

Business at Virginia Cables settled into a new rhythm with Allen at the helm. Allen was now the one working 60 hours per week and doing everything he knew how to keep the business on a steady course. He set up meetings with a few potential customers, but soon got discouraged because they ultimately chose to "go another way." He did not handle the rejection well, so he stopped making those calls.

Without Bob the Hub, the employee spokes received no support, and the wheel began to collapse from the weight of the business load. Sales continued to decline, and unbeknownst to Allen, earnings declined even faster. There were small fires beginning to crop up everywhere, but Allen never saw them.

Customer Service and Sales are where the smoke was seen first. Without training and other investment in employees, service levels began to drop. Customers were the first to notice that. Then competitors began to innovate and offer new products. Soon, market share dropped, revenue dropped, earnings dropped, and so did Bob and Tina's personal income from the business. Now well into retirement, and into their late 60s, Bob and Tina were faced with three common scenarios from which they had to choose.

Bob's Bad Options

First, Bob could un-retire, and again take the reins of his business. But he no longer had a passion for "the Why" that he had when he started his business. He had moved on to new passions, volunteering on the of boards of a few local charities, and spending time with his children and grandchildren. Plus, it would require a great deal of work to rebuild the business, and he realized that he did not want to spend the remainder of his life running a business. Family, health, and friends had all become more important over time. Without the passion or the will, Bob knew this was a poor choice.

Second, he could trade his once-lucrative, now mediocre cash machine, for a lump sum of cash by selling his business. Unfortunately for him, the business showed declines in almost every important financial metric that potential buyers consider when they assess how much risk is associated with a business.

Bob talked with a business broker about selling his business to a strategic buyer. He was informed that declining financial performance, a lack of anything that resembles a management team, a lack of documentation, and a lack of well-defined processes are all major risk factors. With a high-risk assessment, buyers will value a business at a significant discount from when the business was at its peak. Offers will be insultingly low, if they come at all, and will certainly not fund the lifestyle to which Bob and Tina had become accustomed. Bob knew that if he took that path there was significant downsizing in his future.

His third option was to sell the business to an insider, someone who really understands the potential of the business. A key employee who knows how to run much of the business and can learn the rest can be a good exit path. But the broker explained that for that to work well, Bob would have needed to start grooming his successor years in advance. It took Bob 15 years to accumulate all the knowledge he had, and very little of it was captured in operating procedures, operating conditions, handbooks, and guides for employees.

For a sale to Allen to work Bob would have to finance the deal and rejoin the company for several years while Allen received proper training and experience. Bob would no longer be running his company; his role would change into a developmental relationship with Allen.

The goals of this third path were to keep everyone employed, provide Bob with some cash now, and if the business grew Bob's equity stake in the business would grow as well. He may need to cut back his from his former, and anticipated lifestyle, but with some consulting income as a supplement, he could have a comfortable retirement.

Key take-aways

Complacency is The Silent Killer. Here are seven warning signs that you may have fallen into a Complacency Trap.

You take success for granted. You believe that because you have been successful, you will continue to be successful. You want the rewards without the hard work.

You lose focus. You abandon the things that made you successful. You drift away from what you know and do best. You no longer focus on growth, and you have stopped growing.

You fail to evolve. You fail to notice that the world and your competition is changing — and you're not keeping up with the times. Your business plan and goals are obsolete.

You stop listening. You think you know everything — and no one has the courage to tell you otherwise.

You go on defense. You think the "game" is already won. You react to situations rather than pursuing opportunities.

You Lose sense of pride. You lose your passion and get careless. You forget your "Why."

You Ignore the customer. You add costs that don't add customer value; you spend more time in staff meetings than in front of customers; you fail to innovate new products for customers.

To avoid falling into a Complacency Trap:

Create stretch goals. Push your limits. Set ambitious yet realistic goals. Challenge everyone to do better and to be better. As soon as you achieve one goal, set another. It's easier to maintain momentum than to rebuild it once it's lost.

Don't be a know-it-all. Know what you know and what you don't know. It's a strength, not weakness, to seek advice from others.

Welcome fresh ideas. Invite fresh new thinking that challenges your perspective. The truth is, surrounding yourself with yes people is like talking to yourself.

Learn from the best. Never stop growing. Identify best practices and make sure to implement them. But remember, operational effectiveness is not a strategy. Set your strategy first, then implement best practices that complement your strategy.

Compete with yourself. View success as a journey rather than as a destination. Focus on beating your best rather than your competition.

Fight against routine. Embrace change. If it ain't broke, take it apart and make it better.

Look for areas of vulnerability. Ask "what-if" questions to uncover blind spots. Find the cracks in your system.

Look to the future (not the past). Success breeds complacency, and complacency breeds failure.

You must constantly be on guard against complacency. You have the ability to control your situation if you have the will and desire. Are You Complacent?

CHAPTER 3

Employee Engagement

Roadblock #3: If I want it done the right way, I have to do it myself.

> "We choose to go to the Moon in this decade and
> do the other things, not because they are easy, but
> because they are hard; because that goal will serve
> to organize and measure the best of our energies
> and skills, because that challenge is one that we are
> willing to accept, one we are unwilling to postpone,
> and one we intend to win." -John F. Kennedy

State of Engagement

ACCORDING TO GALLUP'S State of the American Workplace 2017 report, approximately 67 percent of U.S. employees are disengaged. It is important to note that the employee engagement score does not mean the majority of the organization's workforce are poor performers. Rather, they are indifferent to the organization. They give their time, but not their best effort nor their best ideas. They likely come to work wanting to make a difference, but nobody asks them for their input or gets them involved to make the organization better.

When an organization gets performance management right, employee engagement will naturally rise. The potential impact on the bottom line is significant. When compared with business units in the bottom quartile of Gallup's database, those in the top quartile of engagement realize 10% higher customer satisfaction metrics, 17% higher productivity, 20% higher sales, and 21% higher profitability. Organizations at the top achieve earnings per share growth that is more than four times that of their competitors.

Gallup found that the effective use of communications strategies, implemented by the top companies, directly correlated to them achieving higher levels of employee engagement and business performance. Performance management and employee engagement clearly matter.

Most businesses rely on annual performance reviews to provide feedback and evaluate performance. While this is a powerful tool, employees are looking for a shared purpose, opportunities to develop, ongoing conversations in a "coaching" manner, and a manager who leverages these strengths, rather than criticize and obsesses over their weaknesses.

Employee Engagement

If you are like most owners, you expect a great deal from your employees. You expect them to work as long as required to complete important tasks. And you expect their work to be mistake-free. You expect them to treat every customer as your friend or family in order to provide the highest in customer service. You expect them to come in on weekends or holidays, to complete an urgent and important project, and you are grateful they rose to the challenge and came to your aid. What you might forget is that employees also have expectations.

Employee Expectations

Employees' expectations, their work ethic, and loyalty to their job will run the gamut from fully engaged to couldn't be bothered. Not every employee will be happy with their job or will forego a weekend outing in order to fulfill the needs of the company. Many just want a paycheck, and you must understand that. You don't have to accept it. But you must understand why that attitude exists, what you can do to change it, and what you should do if your attempt at change is not successful.

Pay only goes so far. Higher salaries are like the bigger house syndrome: Move into a bigger house and initially, it feels roomier, but after a while, you fill all the rooms with new stuff, and larger becomes the new normal. Employees don't automatically perform at higher levels if wages are higher because commitment, dedication, and motivation are not based on pay. No matter how high the salary, if you don't satisfy their emotional and intellectual needs, or you treat them poorly, they won't care - about their jobs or your business.

Reasons for Disengagement

In my experience, over time, employees become disengaged for a variety of reasons:

- No sense of mission. Do you have a discussion with your employees about your mission?
- No Goals. Have you shared your vision of the business with your employees? Do you, and they, have goals and action plans?
- No freedom. Do you allow your employees to use their judgment to accomplish their goals?
- No clear expectations. Do you have clearly documented job descriptions and expectations?
- No input. Does your company culture encourage input and suggestions from employees?
- No future. Can your employees grow into new positions as they grow their skills?
- No fairness. Do you reward and praise similar accomplishments? Do similar violations of company policies result in similar disciplinary actions?

- No connection. People care when you care first. Do you show your employees that you care about them?

Engagement is the extent to which people feel connected and committed to their job, team, and organization. Being connected is most clearly reflected in the emotional ownership people feel. Connected employees care about the success of the team as much as they care about achieving their own objectives.

How to spot disengagement

If you don't trust your employees to do something the right way, you have a problem. It could be a problem employee, or it could be that your employees are not engaged and you are part of the problem. I hear from frustrated owners all the time who tell me that their employees simply don't care about the company or the quality of their work. But worst of all, they feel helpless and stuck, unable to enact true change.

Common behaviors of disengaged employees:

- Absenteeism. Absenteeism involves high rates of frequent and unplanned leave. Most people find it much harder to get out of bed and go to work when they are dreading what's waiting for them when they get there.
- Lack of discretionary effort. Discretionary effort is defined as what people do because they want to, not because they feel obligated to. Disengaged people typically do only what they have to do to keep their job. Some deliberately limit their contributions in silent protest at their unhappiness.
- Absence of teamwork. People who are disengaged will often fail to work well with other people. Those who are engaged will often find their disengaged colleagues frustrating and a roadblock to success. The potential for these frustrations to escalate into conflicts is high.

- Suboptimal productivity. Simply focusing on daily tasks is a challenge for disengaged staff. While they struggle to find energy and focus, their job is not getting done.
- Poor-quality work. Errors, overlooked priorities, and missed deadlines are a few examples of how disengagement affects performance.

The Ultimate Disengagement

The ultimate indication of disengagement is a decision to leave the job. While some people will remain in a role in which they are not happy, most will eventually move on to a better opportunity elsewhere. That may be a more interesting or challenging job, more money, a greater work-life balance, or a better fit with the workplace culture. The reasons people choose to leave are many and varied.

The Advantages of Engagement

When I ask people to describe the best team they were ever a part of, the one in which they were most engaged, had the most fun, and got the best results, they almost always mention a team that demanded a lot. People want to achieve tough goals. We chose to go to the moon not because it was easy, but because it was hard. If they want to do great work that makes a big impact then you have to push them to do more, learn more and produce more than they would if they were left alone. And if they don't why do you want them on your team?

In order to demand a lot, you need to have an environment that clearly defines great performance. You need to be able to show people how that little bit extra is making a difference. It also helps to share some of the rewards of that great work.

The transition from Player to coach

You may find it difficult to transition from getting satisfaction from the work you have accomplished, to getting satisfaction from the work your team has accomplished. On the flip side, there is nothing more demoralizing than a boss who rewrites everything you write, who takes credit for everything you created, or who fails to celebrate the great work that you did.

If you want a really engaged workforce, they need the autonomy to use their skills as effectively as possible to achieve agreed-upon goals. They need to feel like it's up to them, and that they are making a difference. That means that they get the credit when things go well, it means recognition of people's efforts, and it means trusting them to get you there. Your job is to make sure they have the skills and competence that they need by providing the tools and training to succeed. When you do, they will soar.

Coaching/Training

Daniel Goleman popularized the concept of emotional intelligence in his 1995 book *Emotional Intelligence*. He suggested that there are six essential leadership styles. Coaching was one of them and it was shown to have a "markedly positive" impact on performance, culture and the bottom line. At the same time, it was the least-used leadership style. As Goleman explained, "Many leaders told us they don't have the time in this high-pressure economy for the slow and tedious work of teaching people and helping them grow."

Goleman published his research when email was still a blessing, not a curse, globalization was just warming up, and we hadn't yet tethered ourselves to our smartphones. Of course, things have gotten more hectic, more demanding, and we're all stretched more thinly than ever before.

Developing Leaders

There are leaders and there are those who lead. Leaders hold a position of power or influence. Those who lead inspire us to do our best. We follow those who lead not because we have to, but because we choose to. We follow those who lead not for them, but for ourselves. If you want to become a better leader, start leading.

Start with Yourself

Before you can credibly and effectively develop others, you should develop yourself first as someone who leads. Otherwise, you may come across as hypocritical, instead of mentoring. Shaping good behavior starts with role modeling and will also help sharpen your development skills.

Developing Employees

When you develop employees, they become smarter, more productive, they perform at a higher level, and ultimately, make you look like a rock star. Developing employee skills also helps with recruiting and retaining the best employees, and it allows you to delegate so you can focus on the more strategic parts of the job. If you want something done right, don't do it yourself, delegate it to the right employee.

Ask Questions

Coaching questions force an employee to think and figure things out for themselves. Questions can also be revisited after an assignment is completed as a way to reflect back on lessons learned and a way to cement the new knowledge or skill.

Learn How to Delegate

You probably spend time working on activities that are comfortable but do not require your knowledge and skill. Letting go of the responsibilities you enjoy will help you develop your employee's skills and frees up your time, so it's a win-win. But, don't expect your employee to do things the same way you would do them. Your employee may fall at first and need additional instructions, but that's how people learn.

Give Stretch Assignments

Other than a job change, stretch assignments are a great way to learn and develop. As a manager, you're in a position to look for opportunities for your employees that are aligned with their development needs and career aspirations. Don't think about picking the most qualified person for the assignment. Instead, think about picking the right developmental assignment for the person.

Why is Delegating Tasks Important?

Delegating common time-consuming tasks to your employees or contractors is a common practice among business owners. It allows you to focus on more impactful tasks that require your full attention. Learning how to delegate effectively is the key to leveraging yourself and multiplying your value to your company. Delegation allows you to move from what you can do personally to what you can manage. It also gives you the freedom to assign the tasks you don't like to do while keeping the things you do enjoy. Delegation is one of the most important and effective management skills. Without the ability to delegate effectively you will never create enduring value.

Tim's Story

Tim had just survived another round of layoffs at the corporation for which he worked for 16 years. He began to dread that time of year when so many of his co-workers simply stopped coming into the office. He wondered if there was something else out there for him. He attended a franchising seminar, but couldn't see himself starting from scratch at his age. He could, however, see himself taking over an existing healthy business and taking it to the next level. He decided he was ready to stop working for someone else and start working for himself.

He lived a frugal life and had saved enough money in his 401K to fund a substantial part of the purchase of a small manufacturing firm. Blue Ridge Belts made drive belts for printers, copiers, and various industrial equipment that needed small, strong, positive drive belts. It was a small niche for which the company was well known. The year before Tim bought the company it did $3.1 M in revenue.

Tim's skill as a manufacturing manager was noticeable from the start. He implemented new quality control procedures and implemented Standard Operating Procedures and Standard Practices for most products the plant produced. Three years after buying the company Blue Ridge Belts' revenue was at $3.9M and growing.

Tim began to set his sights on growing his business much faster now that he really understood the business and the industry. He knew what was required to gain business with some of the bigger Original Equipment Manufacturers (OEMs) in the industry. Specifications were critical. Price was a major consideration. He could easily capture $5M of business by getting specified on one new design for a popular consumer product, and he was determined to do so.

New Equipment

To be able to compete for new designs, Tim knew he needed high quality, but at low manufacturing cost. To achieve these dual criteria, he realized that he needed the latest process technology that would be faster than his current equipment, require less maintenance, and operate with higher up-time. There was an equipment manufacturer Tim had met at a trade show that had described a process Tim thought would work for his needs. Tim called the rep, and soon Tim and his engineer were working with the design team of the equipment manufacturer to specify the equipment and process that Blue Ridge would use to produce products that would meet OEM specifications.

Finally, the new equipment was delivered, installed, and started up by a team of technicians from the manufacturer. After two weeks the bugs had been worked out, and the equipment was humming along as planned. The new equipment was so efficient that 3 of his 12 operators were no longer needed. Tim agonized over the decision to lay off employees, but he was counting on the cost reduction to pay for the equipment. Reluctantly, all 3 were laid off.

New Business

With a new cost structure in place, Tim spent most of his time visiting with customers to understand their needs. His efforts paid off as he was able to win bids on $3M of new business with new customers. He was ecstatic that his plan was going as well as he hoped it would. But after about 8 months of operating the new lines, the plant was consistently missing its production targets, thereby letting customers down and not meeting cost targets.

Tim and the engineer conducted a thorough investigation. Although the machines were supposedly running 24x7, the investigation revealed that they were only running 65% of the time. The other 35% was spent on maintenance, changeovers and waiting for materials.

Production output was low, rework levels were high, and waste-product was building up at the assembly stations. Tim felt foolish that he had not noticed the problems sooner. He had taken his eye off the plant operations and he was frustrated that the supervisor he hired was not on top of the situation.

The operators were also clearly frustrated. They spent much of their time emptying reject trays and frequently had to stop each machine, open it up and remove the product that had been damaged within it. They were concerned about the amount of waste they were producing at a time when they were being told they needed to be more efficient and keep costs down. They were doing their best, but they did not know how to make things better.

It was about this time that I met Tim at a conference at which I was a speaker. We talked about his business, his frustrations, and his desire for help. He simply did not know what to do. The engineers were tinkering with the new lines, but could not find the problem. I suggested that perhaps a fresh perspective from someone not intimately involved might generate new ideas. Tim was delighted I would take a look at his situation.

Improvement Team

After reviewing the overall situation, we formed a small team that had the authority to do whatever was necessary to find the root cause and offer suggestions for improvement. The team included an experienced operator and an experienced maintenance mechanic, the engineer, and an inspection and testing operator. After training in problem-solving tools, the team set about observing the process from start to finish to clearly define the problems. The improvement team used Cause and Effect analysis to develop a list of possible causes.

Taking measurements and comparing them to optimal soon revealed that there was an insufficient vacuum at the drum where the belts were formed. If the suction was low, the belt would not be properly tensioned, and the belt would be out of spec. The team hypothesized two possible causes; insufficient vacuum generated in the first place or vacuum losses throughout the system. The maintenance team and operators frequently changed the drum heads believing these to be causing a vacuum loss, but this had failed to cure the problem. They had never considered that insufficient vacuum was being generated in the first place.

Solution

Realizing that vacuum losses could also occur elsewhere, the operator crawled the length of the machine, looking, feeling and listening for gaps in the pipework. He discovered several loose connections along the route. Once tightened the improvement in vacuum was noticeable. He also checked, cleaned, and replaced the filters but no further significant change was noted. Once these changes had been made, all the drum heads were replaced at one time and a small improvement was observed.

The maintenance mechanic analyzed the operation of the vacuum generator and discovered that there was a faulty control valve. A replacement valve was ordered and installed, and the vacuum at the generator immediately came into the correct range.

The machines were now able to successfully produce 60 belts per minute which was the design capability. Once the problems were identified and corrected defects were eliminated, changeovers were dramatically reduced, and the equipment was again running at design rates. The plant's output increased to make up the backlog and meet all new orders.

The Challenge

While we were able to focus on solving an immediate equipment problem, I suggested to Tim that there were other problems that aggravated the situation and made it go on far longer than it should have. Almost every employee I talked with was experiencing decreasing morale, and the lack of employee engagement was a concern. Employees were worried that they would be replaced by machines just as their fellow operators had been. There was no incentive for increasing productivity, and there was a demonstrable penalty if productivity was too high.

This was preventing the organization from achieving its strategic goals, objectives, and desired financial results. They did not understand where Tim was trying to take the business, and they were suspicious of what he was doing.

It had been over a year since about half of the employees had received a formal annual performance appraisal. The process the company was using was time-consuming and relied primarily on one individual to deliver numerous performance appraisals. It was a burdensome process. Even in the absence of a formal appraisal, the plant supervisor did not routinely conduct informal feedback to employees to provide encouragement or to challenge them to improve performance.

Tim realized that he had to get his performance management review process established in order to begin to improve business performance.

Key take-aways

Performance management becomes much more useful to the employee and organization if reviews follow ongoing conversations, where expectations can be re-prioritized in real-time so that development can happen throughout the year. This enhances efforts to build a highly engaged workforce to gain a strategic competitive advantage.

There is abundant evidence that employees who are aligned and engaged will make the difference between success and failure in tough times. The critical role of employee alignment and employee engagement can be taken for granted if employees are seen as a production input. Over the past decade or more, lean supply chains and strategic sourcing units have increased the productivity of other production inputs while in many cases, the human factor has remained relatively untouched.

To reap genuine productivity gains, companies need to engage the "heads", "hearts" and "hands" of their workforce. Heart refers to employees being emotionally invested in the organization. They are satisfied, committed and proud. "Head" refers to employees having positive thoughts about the organization. They are enthusiastic and embrace challenges. "Hands" refers to employees translating their positive thoughts and feelings into action.

They go above and beyond the call of duty, apply discretionary effort and share knowledge willingly with colleagues. Engaged employees are much more likely to apply Lean Manufacturing or Six Sigma techniques in a sustained way to continue innovating and improving output levels. They are also much more likely to apply and embrace new approaches in their workplace such as control boards, Pareto analysis, Kanbans, multi-manning of machines, rapid changeovers and similar productivity improvement measures.

The journey to improving employee engagement starts with measurement. There are a variety of ways to do this including interviews, focus groups, questionnaires and employee surveys. Employee engagement should be measured regularly, ideally with a standard instrument that can track changes over time and that can compare company results with comparable organizations.

Getting a good reading on current levels of employee engagement allows companies to make targeted and cost-effective changes where required. In certain cases, a relatively minor issue can be the obstacle preventing employees giving of their best, and once it is known, can be fixed with little time, effort or cost.

Once employee engagement levels are known, intervention initiatives can be directed at specific issues, rather than applying wasteful general solutions that don't address the key issues. Typical solutions include specific communications improvements, leadership development, defining roles clearly, improving team dynamics and aligning rewards more closely with performance.

The Liftoff Zone $5M to $15M of revenue

CHAPTER 4

Product Development Process

Roadblock #4: Developing new products cost me a lot of money and I wound up pulling the plug.

> "Any damn fool can make something complex, it
> takes a genius to make something simple."
> – Pete Seeger, Product Director at Docusign

RUNNING YOUR BUSINESS is a demanding job and managing a new product development might be something you have never done before. You may have some reluctance to engage in an activity that could be quite expensive and is just as likely to be a failure as a big hit. Without experience managing the process, the results tend to be binary. It pays off in a big way, or it is a flop, and flops happen 80% of the time unless you get the process right.

Types of Innovation

From your customer's perspective, ideas that become solutions to their problems are innovative. There are four universally agreed-upon categories of innovation:

1. **Breakthrough Products:** The type of product that most people immediately think about when they think about innovation.

The product may be new to your company or new to the world and often offers a huge improvement in performance, a large reduction in cost, or a leap in technology. Sometimes these products converge technologies so that several products come together to create something new. These products come on strong in the market, then quickly drop to a lower level of performance as other manufacturers catch up. Many of Apple's products in Steve Jobs' era were considered breakthrough products, such as the iPhone.

2. **Incremental Products:** Also known as sustaining products, they often reduce costs, improve existing product lines, reposition existing products in new markets, or are an addition to an existing platform. They generally improve the current product with new generations. Sustaining products are critical in the market because they usually perform pretty well and extend the life cycle of the breakthrough product before they taper off. Profitability is maximized in the incremental product because it generates revenue for future development without incurring huge development costs.

3. **Platform Products:** These products set the basic architecture for a next-generation product. They are larger in scope than incremental products. You may use the basic design of platform products for several products in a family and can satisfy a variety of markets.

4. **Disruptive Products**: These products have a longer initial gestation period upon release, but then have enormous growth. Disruptive innovations are those that offer simple, low-cost solutions to your customers' problems. They disrupt market-leading products by offering low-quality products at a low price, then improving the quality until they capture the mainstream market. For example, when Netflix came out it wasn't a disruptor because customers didn't get the immediate gratification of picking movies at their local Blockbuster store.

However, as Netflix's service improved, shortening the time to deliver movies and eventually streaming them online, they put Blockbuster stores out of business.

Manage the process, not the Development

An innovation process model is critical to saving your company money and time. There are many approaches and models for innovation, depending on the needs of your company. I managed a global B2B new product and new business development organization for 15 years and I have seen process models come and go. I favor a process that:

- Encourages idea generation and protects seedlings, while quickly killing off weeds
- Allows the idea creator the opportunity to lead the process if they have the skills
- Is strategically informed
- Uses a team approach, with every function in the business involved in the process
- Defines exactly what information is needed to move into the next stage
- Generates the information needed to decide on funding the next step

The Stage-Gate model

The Stage-Gate model is a project management approach that divides up the process of developing new products into a funnel system. Once each stage of product development is complete, it passes through a management-approved gate prior to moving on to the next stage. Companies save money by filtering out the weaker ideas while fully supporting the ideas that can have the greatest impact.

In a study in 2010 by the American Productivity & Quality Center (APQC), the Stage-Gate model was the most popular system for new product development in the United States - 88 percent of businesses use some form of it. Originally, Robert G. Cooper developed this eight-step model in the 1980s, boasting a 30 percent cycle reduction time. His research was focused on large businesses, and that is the firmographic where the model has taken hold. The 8 stages include:

- Stage 1: Concept
- Stage 2: Screen the Idea
- Stage 3: Test the Concept
- Stage 4: Business Case Analysis
- Stage 5: Product Development
- Stage 6: Test Market
- Stage 7: Commercialization
- Stage 8: Launch!

The Growth Zone Innovation Process

I have developed the Growth Zone Innovation Process based on the Stage-Gate process but adapted to smaller businesses. Once your company has a product idea, it enters the Concept Stage. To move on to the next stage the innovation team must complete the Deliverables for that stage. There is no guarantee that a project will move on to the next stage. During the Deliverables Review, the team may be recycled in its current stage for better answers, the project may be ended, or it may be funded in the next stage.

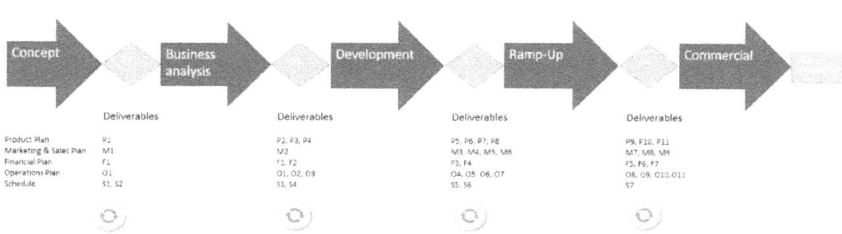

49

Typical Concept stage Deliverables:

- Who is the Ideal Customer?
- What are the product and the compelling reason customers will buy this product?
- How much is the Ideal Customer willing to pay?
- Can the product be made?
- What is the cost target?

At each successive stage of the development, the plan is updated with the additional information that was learned during that stage. The Deliverables of each stage must be tailored to the business, but the general sections that are applicable to most product developments include:

- Product Plan
- Marketing Plan
- Financial Plan
- Operations Plan
- Schedule, project staffing, and the budget

This Deliverables list looks a lot like the outline of a Business Plan, and that is quite intentional. The Deliverables for each successive stage become more detailed as prototypes are built, customer feedback is obtained, and operations become more set. The key is to define the right Deliverables for each stage of the development as they apply to your business.

The business plan format requires the team to look broadly at all functions that are involved in making the development a success. It is designed to ensure that both risks and reward are understood, and decisions are made based on the best available information. You will never have all the answers, and you will always want better information. You must balance the speed of the development with the risk that comes from having incomplete information.

Your innovation process should be as complex as needed, but no more so. If you have never developed a new product, and you are wary of taking that task on, consult with someone with experience. You will save time and money, and you will have a greater chance of success with an experienced person on your team.

How not to do it

One big failure in the annals of product history is Google Glass. Google made a device without considering what problems they were solving for their customers. The product was a monumental (and very expensive) failure.

Fran's Story

RB3 Electronics was founded in 1957 by Roger Bergen 3rd. Roger started RB3 with one product, hearing aids. Later, the link to telephone equipment was easy to make and soon a major telecommunication company became its main customer.

While ownership of RB3 changed on several occasions, the business was successful for each of its owners. However, during the 1980s, with the breakup of AT&T and the loosening of regulations, customers demanded a lower price, higher quality, and product innovation. RB3 profitability declined sharply and the company faced a mounting crisis. It lost its major contracts in the microphone and receiver markets because of sluggishness in implementing new technology in products. It also lost an increasing number of bids based on price and product design.

Several owners tried to revive the company, but none were particularly successful until Fran Johnson came along. Fran was a marketing executive at an IT company based in California. Restructuring at the company where she worked resulted in musical chairs, and when the music stopped, Fran was without a seat.

Fran decided she no longer wanted to work for someone else and decided to move to Virginia to be closer to her aging parents. A UVA grad, she settled in Charlottesville and took a teaching job at the University. She became interested in buying a business, and I helped her buy RB3 in 2006 when revenue was at $5.7M. Fran saw the potential in the company and knew that the key to making it successful again was to launch several platforms for growth. She immediately launched an effort to diversify the customer base by focusing on original equipment manufacturers (OEM) and moving towards product families. By 2015 RB3 was active in four main market segments - telecommunications, mobile communications, home entertainment (TV/video/Hi-Fi) and fire and security - and the company began a period of accelerating growth and increasing profitability. Much of this success arose from a much higher level of new product development (NPD) activity. For example, the two main product categories that were not even in the company's product mix in 2006, currently account for 76% of total sales to an entirely new set of customers.

The New Product Development (NPD) Crisis

Rapid growth through proliferating new products, accelerated by the speed with which many of their key sector markets (such as mobile telephones) were expanding, meant that RB3 began to face a crisis in new product development. Whereas its earlier problems were due to too little development activity, this new crisis resulted from too much unstructured and uncontrolled development.

At the same time, the company faced a series of strategic questions. What categories of products should be manufactured? What markets should be targeted? What portfolio of competencies should be built? Resolution of these questions was essential to provide the strategic umbrella under which NPD could be managed.

Fran knew my experience in NPD and called me for guidance. I interviewed Fran and her management team to better understand their vision, strategy, and goals. It was quickly apparent that work was needed to create a shared vision with clearly articulated goals for the business and a coherent overall business strategy. We worked on the future state vision and setting goals for two months until everyone on the team had a shared vision and clear goals for their functional area. This exercise made it clear that NPD was a core competency that must be nurtured and managed.

To assess the current state of the NPD process individuals and small teams were interviewed to understand the strengths and weaknesses of the current process. We continued the interviews to include every employee to let them know that their ideas were valued.

Our survey identified a number of problem areas within the current NPD system including:

- NPD process unclear
- Ad hoc approach to project selection and priority setting
- Unclear responsibilities and lack of accountability
- Lack of cross-functional involvement
- Inter-function competition rather than cooperation
- No clear link to company strategy in NPD decisions
- No mechanisms for capturing learning from NPD experience

The Growth Zone NPD model was then tailored to the needs of the RB3 business. The team identified the key information that was needed at each management review to decide whether to continue the development or not and the criteria were documented in an NPD manual.

To assess the fit of the process a development that was already underway in an early stage was selected as a test case. The stage-gate process was applied to the development and tweaks to the process were made to better align the intent of the process with the reality of NPD.

Four product developments have been managed using the process since its implementation. One was terminated after the concept stage review for lack of strategic fit. One was terminated after the business case review, and the other two were successfully commercialized and are responsible for over $2.5M in new revenue.

Key take-aways

As your business grows, you will reach a point where selling your current products to your current customers no longer allows you to grow. New ideas will be needed at this point. You need to find ways to tap into new markets, either geographically or demographically. You need to develop new offerings for your customers. Bundling of products and services may offer you new opportunities to build a recurring revenue stream. You cannot expect continued growth by doing what you have always done.

New products are developed to solve problems. You should never start an NPD until you can clearly articulate the problem your target market is grappling with, and why you have a compelling solution to that problem. Don't create another Google Glass.

During your market research phase, you should review the market size and conduct a segmentation analysis. If possible collect data on how people are using current products, how much they will pay, and whether the price for the benefit is reasonable. If you do a lot of hand waving during this early stage, you are setting yourself up for failure later on after spending a great deal of money.

To be successful at developing new products, you need a well-defined process to go from idea to commercialization. The process allows everyone involved in the development to have a shared understanding of the route through the process, and the criteria for go/no-go decisions at each stage. This provides a structure for making a conscious decision when resource commitments must be made.

CHAPTER 5

Financial Management and Control

Roadblock #5: Why do I need to look at these reports? That's why I pay my accountant.

> "Most entrepreneurs come up with a product, or they come up with an idea and they think they can be successful with it. But if they don't know the financial side of their business and understand credit and working capital and what it takes money-wise, you can't be successful. The product is just a product."
> - Tilman J. Fertitta

The Role of Accounting & Finance

ACCOUNTING AND FINANCE play an essential role in the management of any business. Companies operate on money, and if you don't control that money, you don't control your business. By properly accounting for your company's income and expenses, you can manage the flow of money and control the course of your business.

As your business grows, you will probably face a variety of

financial issues. Dealing with these issues early and wisely can lead to profitability. Not dealing effectively with those same issues can cause disaster. Although every company faces its own unique set of circumstances, there are certain issues I have found that all companies in all industries typically grapple with at some time. Issues such as cash flow, cost containment, credit, and debt can all sneak up on you and create havoc. Using proactive methods to deal with common financial issues will help you avoid surprises and stay on track to maximize enduring value.

Understand the data

Financial reports from your accounting system must be rigorously reviewed to spot trends, variances from budgets, and to know what is working and what needs more attention. If your customers are buying more widgets and fewer gizmos, that's something your records can tell you. And if your records tell you you're not getting good enough returns from an outside advertising firm, you can make the decision to change firms, or change tactics. A good strategy will take your business to richer destinations, but a good strategy requires good information.

Analyzing Financial Performance

The key to achieving financial success is asking the right questions so that you are solving the right problems, otherwise, you'll be stuck in an endless cycle of fighting fires and letting the business run you. A good accounting system and a good bookkeeper are essential to your success.

If you can track your revenue and expenses in detail and can tie them to individual jobs, then you can begin to understand which jobs are the most profitable and which are on the low end. Low profitability could be due to a low price, which may be a sales problem, or it could be that costs on the job site were abnormally high. If you capture the data correctly, you will be able to take the appropriate corrective action.

Creating Budgets and Financial Records

By understanding the flow of money through your business you can begin budgeting your anticipated revenues and expenses and use that knowledge to make decisions about how to maintain and grow your business. Budgets are an important element of financial control. You can think of them as roadmaps that allow you to steer your business to greater financial success.

Working Capital

The management of cash flow is one part of a larger management responsibility known as the management of working capital, which refers to the operating liquidity available to an organization.

Working capital is required to ensure that the organization is able to continue its operations and that it has sufficient funds to satisfy operating expenses and any maturing short-term debt. The four factors that affect the amount of working capital available within an organization are:

- Cash
- Inventory
- Accounts Receivable (Debtors)
- Accounts Payable (Creditors)

Cash Flow

Just because you're busy, sales are strong, and the P&L is looking good, doesn't mean you're in good shape. Sometimes a business doing well on paper can find itself short on cash. Many businesses that fail are profitable at the time, but can't pay their bills. The reason for the failure is a shortage of working capital and include the following issues:

- An expanding business spends money on materials (items for sale and salaries) before it completes sales and gets paid. It is a fact of business life that purchases and expenses usually come before sales and profits.

- Capital expenditure, in the form of buying equipment, has an immediate impact on the cash available. Even if the equipment is bought on credit, the monthly payments may seriously drain cash.
- Sales taxes and taxes on profit can both take cash out of an organization and cannot normally be deferred without incurring a penalty of some sort.
- Money may be collected from customers more slowly than expected. This often happens when salespeople are motivated to bring in revenue but have no responsibility for enforcing the payment terms.

Cash flow is a generic term that can be used in different ways depending on the context. It can refer to actual past flows or projected future flows. It can refer to the total of all flows involved or a subset of them—for example, net cash flow, operating cash flow, and free cash flow.

Cash includes all the money the organization has in bank accounts and short-term investments that can quickly be turned into available cash. Cash flow is simply the flow of cash through the organization over time. Cash is paid out in return for the labor and materials that are used to provide goods and services that can be sold. The revenues received provide cash that can then be used to finance further production and sales as well as increasing the organization's economic value.

As an owner, you need to understand how cash flows are generated and what factors impact those flows. This knowledge is an integral part of making financial decisions that increase your company's value.

A Cash Flow Statement

A cash flow statement shows how the final cash balance occurred, how much money flowed in and from where, and how much went out and why. It reflects a firm's liquidity. It includes only inflows and outflows of cash and excludes transactions that do not directly affect cash receipts and payments. This financial statement details three types of financial activities: operating activities, investing activities, and financing activities.

Cash Flow Budget

You need to plan for the known costs and to allow some contingency for unanticipated problems, e.g. late payment by a customer or a supplier withholding raw materials until payment has been processed. This type of planning is referred to as a cash flow forecast and should be part of your overall budgeting process.

Create a cash flow budget to determine when you'll have large bills to pay and when you'll need to borrow cash or use credit to meet your obligations. An organization can have assets and be profitable, but find itself short of liquidity if the assets cannot readily be converted into cash. A line of credit or other business funding can provide the cash needed to start paying your bills and making moves again. Every business does better when it isn't strapped for cash.

Inventory

Your aim should always be to keep inventory as low as realistically possible and to achieve a high rate of inventory turnover. In this way, you are minimizing the impact on your businesses' working capital. In theory, this is ideal to work towards, but in practice, it is more difficult to achieve because you have to meet the commitments you have given to customers.

Accounts Receivable

These are entities that owe your business money. Getting customers to pay in a manner that keeps you afloat is critical to your business' financial health. To avoid liquidity challenges, set clear payment expectations in written contracts, screen customers carefully before extending credit or payment terms, and develop good collections procedures.

Chasing unpaid invoices can be time-consuming and there is a fine line between maintaining a good working relationship with your customers and upsetting them by demanding payment too aggressively. Set expectations at the beginning with customers and be polite but assertive in following through with requests for payment. This is a key area you need to monitor closely to ensure problem payers are identified as soon as possible. To avoid A/R problems:

- Make sure that the payment terms are agreed in advance
- Send out invoices and statements promptly
- Have comprehensive credit policies
- Ask early and ask often, preferably by telephone
- Concentrate on the biggest debts first

Accounts Payable

Many businesses adopt a policy of delaying the payment of suppliers as long as possible. There is an obvious advantage in adopting such a policy as you are effectively getting an interest-free loan from your supplier.

If your organization adopts this policy, then your cash balance will be higher than would otherwise be the case even though slow payments do not affect the net balance of working capital. However, there are also some disadvantages in a policy of slow payment:

- Suppliers will be reluctant to give discounts
- They may treat you as a problem customer and make all of your requests the lowest priority
- If you are always a slow payer there will be less ability for taking longer to pay in response to a crisis
- Within your industry you will quickly gain a reputation as a poor payer and many suppliers may refuse to work with you, making it hard to change suppliers if the need arises.

Many large corporations use their extensive purchasing power to justify paying suppliers after an unreasonably long time. This sort of policy can leave many suppliers with serious cash flow problems. In these circumstances, many suppliers are prepared to offer the maximum possible discount in exchange for guaranteed quick payments, regardless of the size of the order. Your company may be able to obtain the same price as your larger competitors by agreeing to an immediate payment plan with the supplier.

Credit

Many small businesses need credit to stay open. This can include credit cards, lines of credits from commercial lenders, loans and payment terms from vendors and suppliers. If you damage your credit, you risk increased interest payments, and you may lose one or more lines of credit. This can shut you down if you have to wait for customers to pay their bills before you can order materials to make your product.

Growing Pains

Successful businesses can hit a crossroads where to grow and bolster their success, they need more money than they have. Expansion and reinvestment can be costly. If your business hasn't budgeted for this positive eventuality, then you may face the challenges of securing a loan or selling equity to secure the capital it takes to grow your company.

Over-Expansion

When companies are excited about growth, they sometimes buy other businesses or expand into lines of business that are outside their core competence. The resulting investments can cause financial downturn and leave a business with significant loans to repay. Avoid this problem by ensuring that any acquisition is a good fit with your goals, strategy, and core competencies.

Economic Cycles

Sometimes a business can be doing everything right, and the economy takes a turn. Sometimes economic cycles affect specific industries, and other times they create generalized problems for the entire business community. Smart companies plan for fluctuations and build financial reserves for when the unexpected occurs.

Legal Challenges

Businesses get sued -- it's a fact of life and lawsuits can be very costly to defend. Many companies settle unjustified suits because the costs of going to court and fighting are higher than the costs of settlement. Unfortunately, your business has to be prepared for such costs because if caught off-guard, you could end up in a financial crisis. One way that businesses mitigate these problems is through professional liability insurance, which can help you address certain types of legal suits.

Obeying the Law

Good accounting practices have a practical advantage: They keep your company in compliance with the law. Without good accounting, you could violate any number of laws, such as not paying the right amount of taxes. The sloppiness of poor accounting can also cause you to overlook many minor details that collectively keep a business on the level, like carrying out facility improvements to comply with safety laws.

Additionally, if you ever find yourself under legal scrutiny – and many businesses eventually do – having poor financial records can create a lot of unnecessary trouble.

Taxes

Every small business should have a tax plan to reduce its annual payments. How you incorporate, whether you use employees or contractors and what type of benefits you provide all affect your tax burden. Missing quarterly payments or filing late or incorrect returns can result in penalties, fines or an expensive audit. A tax expert can help you plan tax strategies, including the correct incorporation choice for your business and choosing employee benefit plans, such as health savings, flexible spending or 401(k) accounts, to reduce your payroll taxes.

Julio's Story

Julio Castille comes from a long line of entrepreneurs. Daily conversations at the dinner table about business opportunities instilled within Julio a passion to find business opportunities and make them profitable. He would often drive around with his father and grandfather looking at businesses.

From the beginning, Julio had aspirations of creating his own business, which led to the development of strategic goals for his own startup. In 2005, Julio launched Virginia Dental Equipment (VDE), an eBay-style business selling used business and professional equipment on consignment.

Early Years

The business started with the premise that there is a lot of value sitting idle in used equipment in many companies. Julio identified an opportunity to unlock that value either by selling the used equipment for companies on consignment or, buying the used equipment and reselling it to others.

Julio knew there were plenty of marketplaces that provided general transaction-type services. But over the evolution of the company, he learned that the dental industry has special needs. He offered services around disassembly, installation, parts, and repairs that don't apply to general transaction-type services. He decided to build a marketplace and add those services as a` la carte options.

Julio earned revenue through four product lines: (1) selling used dental equipment on consignment: (2) selling used dental equipment which VDE had purchased; (3) shipping; and (4) repairs and installation. In these early years, Julio was very involved in sales and the day-to-day operations of his business and had a good feel for product profitability.

The accounting system Julio used for reporting, compliance and taxation requirements did not contain detailed relevant financial information about any of these product lines. This made it difficult for Julio to determine where the profits were coming from, and how to plan for future business expansion. In addition, as his business grew Julio realized he was beginning to have issues that required more monitoring, communications and performance management.

By 2010, VDE focused on selling a variety of specialized devices within the dental industry and defined its core activity as selling used dental equipment on consignment. Julio's involvement in the day-to-day operations of the business also changed as he took on new reporting and planning responsibilities. At this time, Julio was still managing without financial details on product lines and relied on his "gut" or "instinct" to make operational decisions, rather than spending hours pulling the information from original source documents. Julio felt that he knew his business well enough to run it without detailed accounting and financial numbers because he worked in sales and operations and knew the profit margin on all his products.

Current Situation

By 2015 VDE had 15 employees, $5.9M in revenue, and strategic warehouses located in the mid-Atlantic region. While Julio was making plenty of money, he had dreams of building the business to a much larger scale. He knew it was a matter of time before eBay or some equipment manufacturer got into the business and shut him out. He wanted his business to be the first, the largest, and the best in the marketplace.

However, sales began to flatten out. The early growth in sales was attributed to acquiring all the opportunities in the immediate geographic vicinity. The sales teams now had to travel to other regional locations and beyond just to maintain sales. They spent more time on the road reducing the productive time available to make a sales call, and travel costs increased significantly. This eroded business margins and sales commissions that each salesperson could make. The regional expansion was having a financial cost as well as a cost to the sales team.

As the geographic expansion gained momentum, the logistical issues associated with routing all the equipment through the main warehouse grew as well. Soon the warehouse was full and VDE's shipping and handling staff were stressed. Reaching a piece of equipment that had been sold sometimes required the staff to move several pieces of equipment in order to get to the one they needed.

The first geographic expansion was a test case, and Julio felt it went well enough to expand into other geographic locations. The marketing manager began to research areas that would have opportunities similar to the Tidewater market.

The Banker

Julio approached his local banker to explore the possibility of getting a loan to fund expansion plans. The banker asked Julio many questions that Julio could not answer from instinct or with the information from VDE's accounting system. After Julio left that meeting, he realized for the first time that there was a lot he did not understand about his business. He began to feel a bit overwhelmed and uncertain about his ability to grow his business. Not only was he dealing with the issues of slowing sales growth and limited warehouse capacity, but he was also trying to search for new ways to develop his business for the future.

But the banker's questions made him realize that as the size of the business had grown, he had been less able to identify how specific products, services, and operating processes were performing, let alone ascertain business opportunities. He no longer knew which types of inventory made the most money. He was unsure if he was charging enough for services provided with the inventory. He could not evaluate whether he was achieving his goal of gaining market share in the niche market of used dental equipment. Julio had failed to grow his systems, processes, and capability along with his revenue.

Entrepreneurial Crisis

The situation at VDE is known as an entrepreneurial crisis when a business has grown so large that the owner can no longer control all aspects of operations. When this occurs, the owner/entrepreneur has to transition into a manager who can provide leadership and direction to employees.

Julio realized that if he was to achieve his business and personal goals, he needed someone to mentor him through the changes he would need to make. He called me.

Performance Evaluation to Support Expansion

Julio's accounting system was not the best system on the market in 2005, and the company that sold it to him went out of business. It had been kept operational by various IT freelancers Julio knew. The reporting capability and the amount of data that was stored in the system were both rather limited. The first thing we explored was moving to a new accounting system that could capture the data Julio needed and aggregate that data into useful reports.

After the new system started up, we reviewed the historical earnings performance for the firm as a whole. We still needed to determine:

- How do I evaluate product and service performance?
- What profit margins are the products and services achieving?
- What are my operating costs and what are my fixed committed costs?
- Furthermore, how do I know how the business is doing relative to its competitors?

Julio and VDE's accountant added information to each purchase and sales transaction recorded in the accounting system which identified product line. The next task was to convert VDE's financial statements and sales units into the variable costing or contribution margin format. Total revenue was broken up by product and service sales lines and matched with the corresponding variable costs to calculate product and service line contribution margins.

We then prepared a budget for 2016. I showed Julio how to compare actual performance with expectations by showing both the budget and the historical figures on the same report and calculating the variance between the two. Knowing the difference between the actual and budget line items is important, but knowing what caused the variance is even more important.

Usually, variances can be explained by the difference between the actual price sold and cost paid for each product and service and what was budgeted or expected at the time of setting the financial goals. But variances can also be explained by the difference between the actual quantity of product and service that was sold and what was budgeted or expected at the time of setting the financial goals.

I showed Julio how to prepare a flexible budget which included a volume-adjusted column. This new column allows for variance calculations that separate the effects of selling price and purchasing costs from sales and purchase quantities for each product and service line item. Favorable or unfavorable price and volume variances will guide investigations to answer questions such as:

- Did we lower prices due to competitive pressure, or was it because of discounts on old products to entice customers?
- Were our costs up because purchase costs were up or because we sold more this year?
- If we performed 8% better than our budget, is this good or bad performance given our competitors in the marketplace?
- Which product or service contributed most or least to our overall performance this year?

Julio used the variance analysis and other reports to support operating decisions that would allow VDE to maintain profit margins. The information also helped with strategic decisions about its products and services. Julio identified products and services that were not performing well and determined whether there was a cost overrun or whether it was time to retire the product or service in favor of new products and services.

We then reviewed information compiled by the sales manager at VDE, who tracks competitor information through networking, searching the internet, reading business publications, discussions with clients, and gets published numbers from information provided by a professional association of companies selling new and used dental equipment to which VDE belongs.

Julio has transformed himself and his business since his meeting with the banker. He now spends 20% of his time working on strategic matters of importance to his business. Today, his business, Virginia Dental Equipment (VDE), has grown into the dominant player in the niche market of sales of used dental equipment. Based in Tidewater Virginia, the business continues to grow at double digits each year.

Key take-aways

Ensure your accounting system is set up properly to provide you with the information you need to control your business. Keep your books up to date. That means processing all transactions in a timely manner. In today's computerized world, this process is as simple as making sure software is connected and you are collecting revenue and expenses as they occur. If you haven't embraced a good accounting software package, this should be your first step. Next, have an experienced bookkeeper set up the accounts for you. If your accounts are not set up properly, you will not be able to create reports that are useful to you. Once properly set up, the software will allow you to keep your books current, enabling you to analyze your situation and spot any problems so they never become a crisis.

Pay attention to your financial reports. If you need help to set up your books, manage your accounts, understand and keep current on all tax laws, and grasp what your financial statements are telling you, then seek help. Don't let your business gets stranded on the side of the Growth Zone highway.

Understand how cash comes into your business and how it is used. This information can be easily reviewed by learning to read and analyze your company's statement of cash flow. Knowing how cash comes into your business (sources) and how cash goes out of your business (uses) is how successful businesses flourish and why countless businesses fail.

Ultimately, you want profit to be your No. 1 source of cash. That will probably require growing your sales beyond their current level. As a company's sales increase, operating accounts such as accounts receivable and inventory increase too. This detail is often missed because this use of cash doesn't appear as an expense on your company's profit-and-loss statement, but rather as an increase in the balance of those accounts documented on a balance sheet. When missed, this use of cash can have devastating results.

Don't delegate financial management controls. According to the Association of Certified Fraud Examiners, an average company loses 5 percent of its sales to fraud each year. With most small businesses averaging less than 4 percent profit per year, this can be the difference between success and failure.

Some important controls to have in place include segregation of duties. The employee paying the bills should not be signing the checks, and the check signer must inspect the supporting documentation for validation. In addition, having passwords in place for access to accounting software, periodic oversight of inventory counts and documentation, and a systematic review of bank statements along with reconciliations are highly recommended.

While financial mistakes and bad practices can lead to failure and financial ruin, good financial controls can be your ticket to success.

CHAPTER 6

Customer Satisfaction

Roadblock #6: Customer Satisfaction is close to 100%. I don't need to make any changes.

> "If you take care of your people, your people will
> take care of your customers and your business will
> take care of itself." - JW Marriott

Customer Loyalty and Engagement

EVERY BUSINESS OWNER agrees that having loyal customers is key to business success. The question is do you ensure customer loyalty or do you do your best and hope for the best. Some owners I have talked with have taken steps to implement a loyalty and rewards program. Some point to their monthly newsletter or discount program to demonstrate their efforts. All of these are good starts. However, they are not enough. They may make an impact, but creating customer loyalty is something that must be front and center in your company. If you do not measure customer loyalty and take steps to ensure you are delighting your customers you may have experienced some issues noted below:

- 95% of customers will take action after a negative experience by sharing concerns with friends and family, or churning.
- 91% of unhappy customers will not willingly do business with you again.
- 84% of customers who leave, do so because of poor service.
- 70% of the reason customers leave has nothing to do with the product.
- 67% of consumers list bad customer experience as the primary reasons for churning.
- Each year the average company loses 10-15% of its customer base.
- 4% of dissatisfied customers will complain—the other 96% leave, 91% for good.
- It costs 5 to 10 times more to attract a new customer than to keep an existing one.
- You will never hear from most customers who leave you.

Yes, you need a great product. Yes, you need a competitive price. But the customer experience surrounding your product or service, through each stage of your sales funnel is now a key differentiator between your business and your competitors. It comes down to how your customer experiences your brand and how that brand makes them feel. In essence, their satisfaction with your brand, your product, your service, your messaging, and more, will make or break you.

Ongoing satisfaction leads to loyalty. Once customers have placed trust in your company and are assured that you will continue to deliver, they will continue to do business with you. Loyalty is a worthy goal. Loyal customers are worth up to 10 times their initial purchase value. A recent study showed that companies that strategically step away from price wars to concentrate on customer experience metrics are experiencing more retention and better growth.

Fundamental Concepts

Three fundamental concepts lay the foundation that allows you to create loyal customers.

Satisfy your customers with quality

Customers want defect-free products and services. You must design your product and service so that it can be expected to function perfectly within foreseeable boundaries. Things will sometimes go wrong. Your products and people will sometimes fail due to unpredictable circumstances. But a sloppy or incomplete product or service design is, from a customer's perspective, intolerable.

Your ideal customer has expectations of product quality that come from many sources, including previous quality levels set by your business, value propositions set by your competitors, and impressions gleaned from friends, family, and the media.

Satisfaction is the difference between your customers' expectations and service delivery. It is imperative that you know your customers' expectations and that you are prepared to change your product or service to deliver what your ideal customers want. This is basic business blocking and tackling, but it is ignored far too often. Product quality begins with truly understanding the needs and desires of your ideal customer.

Enticing customers with a highly discounted price in order to buy something that does not fully meet their needs may produce a one-time sale, but it does not create customer loyalty. Companies try all sorts of loyalty and sales gimmicks, but ignore the fundamental business concept of a balanced transaction. Customers give you their hard-earned cash and expect something of equal or greater value in return. If your product does not meet all your ideal customers' needs and expectations, you will never create loyalty. While your business might survive with disappointed, single-purchase customers, only businesses with a focus on customer satisfaction will thrive.

Go out of your way to resolve problems

Even the most carefully thought out service delivery processes will fail on occasion. Service breakdowns and other problems experienced by customers are crucial emotional moments in a business relationship. Be acutely responsive to customer questions, comments, and complaints.

Solving problems will have a big impact on your business success and that's why you need an effective problem resolution process. An effective process does not simply restore the situation to the pre-problem status. Effectiveness is measured by whether you have restored customer satisfaction. Customers who care enough to complain are often your most loyal customers.

Resolve a service problem effectively and your customer is more likely to become loyal than if she'd never run into a problem in the first place. Until a problem occurs, the customer doesn't get to see us fully strut our service. Of course, I would never recommend that you intentionally make mistakes so you can engineer a splendid recovery and win yourself some client love in the process. But there is a silver lining to keep in mind when you're staring down a problem.

Engage your customers by reaching out to create a dialogue

Providing your customers with an open channel for communication and feedback engages your customers and strengthens your relationship with them. Engaged customers are more satisfied, more loyal, and more likely to promote your company than unengaged customers. They go out of their way to show their association with your company. An engaged customer also supports you during both good and bad times, because they believe what you're offering is superior to what your competitors have to offer.

Engagement takes your customers beyond passive loyalty to become active participants and promoters of your product. Engaged customers will want to give you more feedback – and you better be ready to listen to it and respond accordingly. The result will be engaged customers who will spend more money with you over time.

So how do you become a company that actively engages its customers? Follow these simple rules:

- Listen to customer feedback from comment cards, letters, phone calls, and surveys
- Respond quickly and personally to concerns of high interest to your customers
- Organize unstructured feedback for tracking and trending over time
- Trust your customers when they tell you there is a problem
- Use statistical techniques to discover which action items will have the most impact on your business outcomes

Five Common Customer Experience Metrics

You can't know whether or not you are successful unless success is defined and measured. With a clearly established metric for success, you can quantify progress and adjust your process to produce the desired outcome. Without clear objectives, you're stuck in a constant state of guessing. There are five common metrics businesses use to assess how well they are satisfying their customers.

1. NPS – Net Promoter Score
2. CES – Customer Effort Score
3. CSAT – Customer Satisfaction Score
4. Five Star Reviews
5. Churn rate

These five metrics are used to measure one of three things: Loyalty, Satisfaction, or Quality. The key is knowing which one of these things you want to measure.

- To measure loyalty, use NPS or CES.

- To measure satisfaction, use CSAT
- To measure quality, use 5 Star Reviews

Loyalty and satisfaction correlate with growth. Since I am foremost interested in helping you grow enduring value, let's look at the customer experience metrics that measure loyalty and satisfaction. Customer satisfaction score (CSAT) is the average rating of your customer's satisfaction with a particular interaction or process, the net promoter score (NPS), indicates the probability that a customer refers a brand to another person, and the customer effort score (CES), indicates how easy it is for a customer to do business with you. These customer satisfaction metrics are then used to estimate consumer behavior.

NPS: The Standard for Measuring Customer Loyalty

Many companies today recognize the power of loyalty and its impact on financial performance. Not only is the notion of loyalty intuitively appealing, but a growing body of empirical evidence suggests that companies that choose to ignore loyalty may find themselves experiencing the issues noted at the beginning of this chapter.

Despite the growing popularity of loyalty programs, the true value of such programs is often not realized due to ambiguous or ill-defined measurement systems. Satmetrix, in close consultation with Frederick Reichheld, founder of the Loyalty practice at Bain & Company, embarked on an independent research project in 2003. The objective was to better understand the micro- and macro-economics of customer loyalty. At the micro-level, the research focused on finding a loyalty question that could consistently predict short-term purchase and referral behaviors. At the macro-level, the goal was to validate this metric by linking it to long-term corporate financial indicators.

The results of this investigation were compelling. Not only did Reichheld and Satmetrix discover the most effective question for accurately measuring customer loyalty, but they also identified "Net Promoter Score" as a valuable tool for assessing long-term corporate growth.

A single loyalty question is sufficient to gauge customer purchase and referral patterns across seemingly disparate industries. Specifically, the 'likelihood to recommend' question proved to be highly correlated to actual customer behavior 80% of the time. If customers reported that they were likely to recommend a particular company to a friend or colleague, then those same customers were also likely to actually repurchase from the company, as well as generate new business by referring the company via an online review. Conversely, if customers reported that they were not likely to recommend a company, they were also less likely to engage in actual repurchase or referral behaviors.

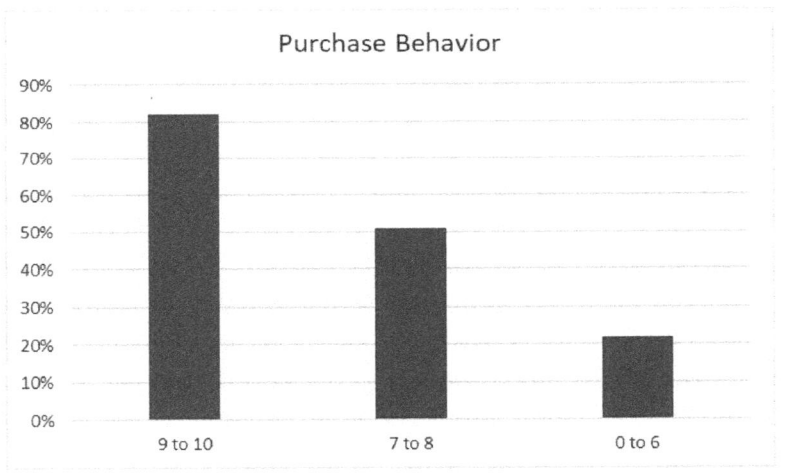

NPS consists of one question: "How likely are you to recommend our company to a friend or colleague?" Respondents answer using a 0-10 scale, with 10 being "Very Likely" and 0 as "Very Unlikely."

The 0-10 scale makes it easier for you to segment customers according to their responses: Those that fall into:

- 0-6 are called Detractors. They are unhappy customers who will spread bad word of mouth and post bad reviews about your brand
- 7 and 8 are Passives. They are customers who are relatively neutral about your brand
- 9 and 10 are Promoters. They are the customers who love your brand and will tell others about it

How to Calculate NPS

To calculate your NPS score, you need to subtract the percentage of Detractors from the percentage of Promoters.

Depending on how many and what kind of answers you get, your NPS score can be anywhere in the -100 to +100 range. This is not like a school exam grade where anything under 60 is failing. Still, anything less than 0 is a bad sign. A score between 0 and 30 is a good score, a score between 30 and 70 is a great score, and anything over 70 means you have very high loyalty levels.

NPS is a one-question framework that gives you the right insight to help you understand your customers' experience and make impactful business decisions. In addition, you can (and should) include an open-ended question afterward, like a simple "why did you give us that score?" This can give you even more insights.

The beauty of NPS as a customer experience metric is that it is a short survey that is easy for customers to complete. It can be sent in a wide variety of channels — email, web, SMS, etc. And it can be integrated with your CRM to readily and easily trigger surveys to go out at important moments.

Customer Effort Score (CES)

To examine the links between customer service and loyalty, the Customer Contact Council (CCC), a division of the Corporate Executive Board, conducted a study of more than 75,000 people who had interacted over the phone with contact-center representatives or through self-service channels such as the web, voice prompts, chat, and e-mail. The CCC also held hundreds of structured interviews with customer service leaders and their functional counterparts in large companies throughout the world. The research addressed three questions:

- How important is customer service to loyalty?
- Which customer service activities increase loyalty, and which don't?
- Can companies increase loyalty without raising their customer service operating costs?

Two critical findings emerged that should affect your customer service strategy. First, delighting customers doesn't build loyalty. Second, reducing their effort, the work they must do to get their problem solved does. Acting deliberately on this insight can help improve customer service, reduce customer service costs, and decrease customer churn.

Why is CES a Customer Experience Metric?

Studies show that 96% of customers with a high-effort service interaction become more disloyal compared to just 9% who have a low-effort experience. If measuring loyalty is the goal, then you need to take into account the effort it takes for customers to interact with you. This measurement is quick and easy for customers to evaluate, and it's simple to implement across different service and survey channels. CES correlates with business outcomes and is easy to track over time.

Trying Too Hard

According to conventional wisdom, customers are more loyal to firms that go above and beyond and "delight their customers". But the research shows that exceeding customer expectations during service interactions by, for example, offering a refund, a free product, or a free service such as expedited shipping makes customers only marginally more loyal than simply meeting their needs. You don't need to delight your customers; you need to make it easy for them to do business with you.

Make It Easy

When it comes to service, you create loyal customers primarily by helping them solve their problems quickly and easily. Framing the service challenge as "making it easy for the customer" can be highly illuminating, especially if you have been struggling to delight your customers. Telling frontline reps to exceed customers' expectations is apt to yield confusion, wasted time and effort, and costly give-aways. Telling them to "make it easy" gives them a solid foundation for action.

There are three common complaints about service interactions that focus specifically on customer effort. Customers resent having to contact the company repeatedly (or be transferred) to get an issue resolved, having to repeat information, and having to switch from one service channel to another (for instance, needing to call after trying unsuccessfully to solve a problem through the website). You can re-duce these types of effort and measure the effects with the Customer Effort Score (CES), which assigns ratings from 1 to 7, with 7 represent-ing very high effort.

CES Question

Customer Effort Score (CES) is a single-item metric that measures how much effort a customer has to exert to get an issue resolved, a re-quest fulfilled, a product purchased/returned or a question answered. CES is typically indicative of customer loyalty. CES surveys typically ask the question, "on a scale of (1) very easy to (7) very difficult, how easy was it to interact with your company. The research shows that customers are more loyal to a product or service that is easier to use.

Customer loyalty is tied to the amount of effort customers expend when interacting with your brand. This customer experience metric measures that effort and its effect on your customers. This allows you to evaluate and take the necessary actions according to the survey data to make your customer interactions easier.

How Does Customer Effort Score Work?

Companies who use this metric are hoping to reduce the effort it takes for their customers to interact with a call center, website ordering process, or to leave a review. They choose the interaction they want to understand and send out a single question. An example is: "To what extent do you agree or disagree with the following statement: The company made it easy for me to (e.g. return a product)."

There is a scale from (1) Strongly Agree to (7) Strongly Disagree.

Surprisingly, there was not much difference in loyalty between those who responded with a 1, 2, or 3. Expending the effort to move a customer from a 3 to a 1 is not likely to have a large business impact. In contrast, moving those customers who responded with 4-6 up to a 3 can make a large impact on revenue and profitability. You don't have to delight your customers, but you must make it easy for them to do business with you. That is how you build enduring value.

When to Use Customer Effort Score

- Immediately after an interaction with a product that led to a purchase or subscription. For example, immediately after a touchpoint with customer service or after an important product or service touchpoint like signing up for a trial.
- Immediately after an interaction with customer service such as after an email support ticket has been resolved or perhaps even after they read a knowledge base article to determine how effective it was in resolving the issue.
- To measure the aggregate experience someone has with your product or brand in general, but because the question implies a discrete and isolated user experience, it is most often used to measure service or product level issues.

What Is Customer Satisfaction?

Whether you're in a B2B or B2C marketplace, you're living in an H2H world, Human to Human. And that's where the importance of customer satisfaction comes in.

Broadly speaking, customer satisfaction is exactly what it sounds like, how satisfied are your customers? It indicates the fulfillment that customers derive from doing business with your company. Customers derive satisfaction from a product or a service based on whether their need is met effortlessly, in a convenient way that makes them loyal to your business. Customer satisfaction measures how your product, service, and overall experience either falls short, meets, or exceeds customer expectations. Customer satisfaction is an important step to gain customer loyalty.

Why Is Customer Satisfaction Important?

If you don't measure customer satisfaction, you will have no way to identify unsatisfied customers. Some will be bashing you on social media, and hopefully, you will notice these former customers and deal with the issues that drove them to share their review of you online. But what about the ones who are quietly unsatisfied and instead of complaining will just take their business elsewhere?

If you are not talking to your customers and finding out areas of your customer journey that are causing issues, then you will not be able to make important improvements. Customer satisfaction surveys allow you to analyze customer feedback and make changes to improve your service, website, product and more. You also won't be able to identify your happy, satisfied customers who could go on to become advocates for you and provide you with valuable insight into where you are performing well.

Engaging your customers allows you to gather the data to determine what is going right and what needs some improvement. That leads to process changes that result in more satisfied customers. Satisfied customers are a good thing because they buy more and stay with you for a longer time. If you prioritize customer satisfaction, you will grow and increase revenue. Your business will be stronger, and you will be building a business with enduring value.

Benefits of Customer Satisfaction

The research strongly shows the correlation between loyal customers and financial performance of companies across a wide variety of industries.

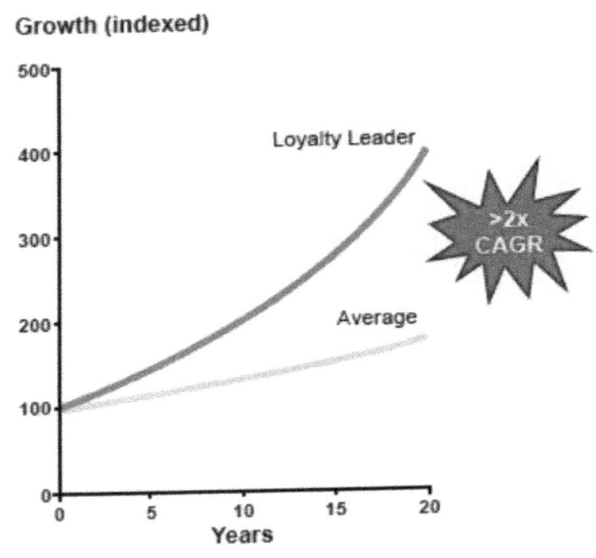

Companies that have loyal customers experience much greater growth than companies that have an average level of satisfaction for the industry. If you actively work to increase customer satisfaction, you're more likely to see an increase in revenue.

There are many other reasons to make customer satisfaction a top priority. In our ultra-connected and always-on digital world, your customers can instantly share their experience with a brand with thousands of others on social media and review sites like Yelp. A bad review can go viral and do considerable damage to a brand's reputation.

You also need to consider how customers' trust and seek out online recommendations:

- 93% turn to online reviews to decide if a business is good or bad
- 92% of consumers trust recommendations from friends and family
- 74% of consumers listed word-of-mouth as a key influence in their buying decision
- 68% of respondents said a positive review made them more likely to use a business, while 40% said a negative one made them not want to use it
- 48% of consumers won't consider a business with less than a 4-star rating
- 34% read 4-6 reviews before deciding to trust a business
- Facebook and Yelp are the two most trusted review sites.

That's a lot of potential goodwill and positive publicity. But it works both ways. Consumers who have a bad experience share that bad experience with others 60% of the time– and they tell 3x as many people – compared to only 46% who share the good ones.

Measure Customer Satisfaction

Without any data or opinions to work from you won't know what is upsetting your customers and what you are doing right. There are a number of different ways to analyze and measure how satisfied your customers are and these surveys are cleverly called customer satisfaction surveys or CSAT. Customers are able to express their satisfaction, or dissatisfaction with the service, product, transaction or interaction with a company.

This is often done using one main question – how satisfied are you with your product and/or service? You ask your customer to give you a rating between 1 to 5, (or 1 to 7, 10 or 100) on how satisfied they were with your service or the particular area of customer satisfaction you want to measure. Your average rating will give you an idea of where you are now. Collect more insight through open follow-up questions to delve deeper into why the customers provided that rating and you are now on your way to creating a better experience for your customers, leading to increased loyalty and improved profits. Customer Satisfaction surveys can be used in a number of different scenarios such as

- Customer Support Satisfaction: One of the most popular use cases is to trigger customer support satisfaction surveys after an interaction with your support team. You might think an issue is resolved but how satisfied is the customer with that resolution?
- Product Satisfaction: Get feedback on your products so you can make adjustments to improve sales and get inspiration for new product ideas.
- Sales Satisfaction: Learn more about how you won a sale or how likely a customer is to buy from you again. Sales satisfaction surveys can also help you understand how competitive you are in the market and can provide insight into future purchase behavior.
- Website Satisfaction: Is your website delivering a good experience? A Website satisfaction survey can identify pain points in your online experience and help you to deliver a better customer journey.

Improve Customer Satisfaction

There are some universal ideas that can be applied across most companies that should lead to improved customer satisfaction but the best ideas will come from your own customers. Every company is different with each industry having its own set of competitors and customer expectations. Look at what your customers are telling you and identify points in your customer journey that are leaving your customers unsatisfied. Once you identify and fix these issues, you can see how this impacts your CSAT rating and continuously measure and improve as you move forward.

When you begin to look at the customer experience as a series of processes that must be continually revised as technology, products, and customer's needs change, you will begin to see possibilities open up for you.

Contrary to Popular Opinion, Customer Service is NOT a Thing of the Past!

Product and price are certainly key differentiators in the minds of customers, but the way to a customer's heart is through people providing outstanding service. Outstanding service providers cultivate strong and meaningful relationships with customers from the first contact, whether by phone or face to face. They know how to listen; they smile, and they are sincere. It just takes a few intentional steps, followed every day, to turn good service into sales.

Customer Service as Sales

You may have a potential sales force you have not considered. This sales force speaks to your customers regularly and helps them each time. They may already have great relationships built with your customers. Most importantly, their relationships are built on trust. It's the customer service department. There's only one problem: they don't think of themselves as salespeople and as a result, are simply reactive, rather than proactive.

Tapping into this unmined resource can produce incremental topline revenue. Unfortunately, it's not as easy as simply saying "Sell!" Training and education are required to nurture and guide your customer service team to follow sales best practices and lay the groundwork for growing your business without adding to your headcount or your overhead.

The reason many CSRs choose customer service over sales is that they see salespeople as pushy, sleazy or self-serving. They may also be uncomfortable dealing with what they consider awkward "sales" conversations, and they don't know how to handle or avoid push back. When they accept that there's another way to sell that actually helps customers make smart buying decisions, they will move past this stereotypical view and be more comfortable in a sales role. Service providers are born to help. When they see sales through that lens, they'll be open to the role. A step-by-step process takes the pressure off them and your customer.

Engage customers at a deeper level

When you ask customers about their problems, their thoughts, and their challenges, you tap into their wants and needs. Ensure your customer service providers are trained and empowered to craft compelling questions and are actively listening to your customers.

The surface problem a customer presents with is rarely the real problem. More likely the presenting problem is merely a symptom, or an excuse to avoid discussing the real problem. When this happens, the issue is usually a lack of trust. Until you establish trust with your customer, a sale will not happen. One way to establish trust is by exploring deeply to find out what's behind the visible issue. Only then can your CSR match your products and services to solve the real issues.

Sell Value

When your CSRs understand the difference between value and price, they will stop assuming that buyers only want the lowest-priced items. They can start exploring needs and will match those needs to the right product. Customers need a return on their investment, and a customer service provider's product knowledge, experience, problem-solving abilities, and industry knowledge have huge value.

Susan's Story

Virginia Wireless (VW) is the pseudonym for the operator of wireless retail stores throughout Virginia. It was created through the merger of several independent dealers and consists of 21 retail stores. Prior to the merger, each dealer had its own culture, and its own operating systems and processes. The first challenge for VW was to create a single, cohesive entity with a consistent set of business processes.

As a dealer, VW was tied to the pricing, product, and positioning of the brand it carries. The primary independently controllable marketing element for the company is the customer service and selling skills of its people. Throughout the network, the knowledge and skill of the retail sales force varied widely.

To address these challenges, I was retained to help Susan, the VW CEO, to create a strong, consistent customer service and sales culture introduced as the VW Way. After the first full year of implementation, the VW Way has resulted in dramatic changes in both the consistency of sales and service and financial results. The program was implemented in five distinct stages, outlined below.

Stage One – Assessment

If you don't know where you are, you can't map out how to get where you want to go. Therefore, the first stage of any business improvement project is to obtain a baseline of performance.

Needs Assessment/ Gap Analysis

Working with Susan and her senior and regional management teams we assessed the performance levels of staff throughout the company to obtain a baseline of performance. The assessment included reviews of all existing business practices and operational policies. We particularly focused on the processes that impacted customer touchpoints. A subsequent gap analysis identified the high-yield opportunities for growth and development. Key performance and financial metrics were established to evaluate the ongoing impact of changes introduced.

Initial Performance Standards

Susan and her senior team then developed a preliminary set of behavioral performance standards for front-line employees and managers and a methodology for tracking execution of those standards.

Managers' Roles Redefined

It was immediately clear that the role of store managers needed to be redefined to be responsible for the continuous improvement of their teams. Although managers still retained their administrative functions, their main responsibility was daily coaching and mentoring of the store staff. Regional managers were given the responsibility to continuously train the store managers.

Stage Two - Customer Service Training Rollout

Prior to rolling out the new customer service training to front-line employees, regional managers and store managers participated in extensive training to provide them with the skills for coaching and motivating their teams. This program showed managers how to set daily performance goals, observe live interactions, assess performance levels, and respond appropriately. The training focused on changing the existing feedback coaching paradigm to a more effective, proactive, forward-looking approach to anticipate and prevent problems before they occurred.

Regional managers participated in an additional intensive five-day train-the-trainer program to ensure that store managers received ongoing coaching in delivering the VW Way. Regional managers were tasked with ensuring that every employee in their region understood and followed the VW Way. Over the course of two months, all employees received training in the VW Way. The program was focused on core customer service skills and behaviors.

Live Environment Coaching

Immediately following the training, VW regional manager/coaches spent a full day in each location, working with the staff and managers to help them execute the skills in the live environment. During this time, employees were evaluated to ensure their understanding and retention of The VW Way.

Stage Three - Program Support

To provide ongoing support a web-based assessment tool was created. The purpose of the tool was twofold: First, to assess retention of the skills and principles; and second, to encourage employees to revisit the key elements of the training. This was rolled-out one month following the live environment coaching. The assessments were scored by management, and feedback was provided to each employee.

VW Manager/Coaching Log

A coaching log was created for all managers to complete on a weekly basis, outlining their coaching efforts for the coming week. A process was established for review and response to activities placed in the log by store managers and regional management.

VW Coach follow-up

After the second stage of the training was completed, Regional manager/coaches regularly visited the stores, to provide coaching in the VW Way.

Biweekly Support Tools

Every two weeks, store managers received new skills drills and other activities to share with their teams. This kept the momentum of The VW Way alive and ensured that the skills continued to be used in the live environment.

Stage Four - Raising the Bar

Once it was clear that there was sustained traction with the existing employee behavior expectations, the company narrowed the focus to mandate and drive the highest yield behaviors. The measurement tools were adjusted, along with the compensation plan, to reflect this change.

Compensation Alignment

The company implemented a company-wide change to compensation with a sliding scale of bonuses based on monthly measurement of service and sales behaviors. This was specifically targeted at managers and was structured to encourage them to proactively drive the behaviors in their locations.

Stage Five - High-Intensity Relentless Support

To demonstrate the full potential of the VW Way, each VW regional manager/coach selected one location as a dedicated pilot site. Each coach was embedded in their location for a one-month period. This was a high-intensity initiative to see the effect when the VW Way was executed consistently at the highest level. During the month, regional manager/coaches interacted with store managers and employees following each transaction throughout the day. They did not provide feedback but instead implemented a proactive, motivational feed-forward approach. They created a strategic performance development map for each employee to ensure their coaching efforts were focused and effective.

Results of the initiative were measured weekly, with the year-over-year gross margin results of the Pilot stores being compared to the overall company average. The results of the program were startling. By the end of the second week, Pilot stores were exceeding the gross margin average for the company by over 40%. This trend continued throughout the program. Following the tremendous success of the pilot project, the initiative was rolled out to the remaining stores. The results were consistent with the initial pilot, with gross margin increases as high as 53%.

Conclusions

The VW Way initiative illustrates three key conclusions:

Growth Opportunities Are Greater Than You Think

Most organizations do not envision that the opportunity exists for a dramatic change in business results. Business plans that project ten or twenty percent increases in profitability are often viewed as idealistic or unattainable. This example illustrates that the opportunity for growth can be far greater than imagined when a company makes a commitment to changing the way it does business.

Customer Service Training Impacts Business Results

Customer service training has historically been referred to as a 'soft skill.' This is largely due to the difficulty in attaching any real cause-and-effect benefit to improvements in business results. The VW Way initiative was able to show a direct and significant correlation between improved customer service performance and business results.

Behavior Change Requires Relentless Support

The dramatic improvement in customer service performance and business results from the pilot component of the program highlights the impact of a high-intensity approach to change.

Key Takeaways

Customer experience (CX) and Employee experience (EX) are now two of the driving forces of business. Independently, each function leads to valuable relationships with customers and employees but when CX and EX are managed together, they create a unique, sustainable competitive advantage.

You'd better do your best to ensure each customer interaction is a positive one. If you don't place a premium on relationship marketing and customer satisfaction, you won't be aware of problems or complaints until it's too late.

CHAPTER 7

Leadership

Roadblock #7: I'm not sure that my team has the right skills to run the business without me.

"I am not afraid of an army of lions led by a sheep,
I am afraid of an army of sheep led by a lion."
-Alexander the Great

Not the right team

AS YOUR BUSINESS grows, you may promote current employees into positions of greater responsibility. A compromise between simply adding responsibility and giving a promotion is to offer a stretch assignment. Stretch assignments are a great way of testing an employee's readiness for additional responsibilities and challenges. These added responsibilities provide employees a safe space in which to grow their knowledge, skills, and abilities without a fear of negative consequences if things don't go perfectly.

Whether you hire someone for the position or promote from within, you must feel comfortable with the capability of each manager to grow their functional area consistent with your business plan. If your business has stopped growing, you may have the wrong people on the bus, or you may have the right people in the wrong seats. Either way, you need to proactively make the changes needed to ensure you have the team in place that can accelerate your growth.

If you, or your team, are not performing up to your expectations, you have the responsibility to determine the cause of this failure and to correct it. The following are indicators of ineffective management that must be dealt with promptly before the culture you are building becomes toxic.

Managerial Inadequacy	
Lack of planning	Ignoring customers' needs
Ineffective staffing	Ignoring competition
Poor communication skills	Failure to diversify customer base
Failure to seek or respond to criticism	Failure to innovate
Failure to learn from past failures	Ineffective marketing strategies
Lack of revenue growth	Low employee engagement

Begin by documenting your business plan and holding your managers responsible for achieving the plan within their area of functional expertise.

Recognize your limitations

First-time business owners may lack the knowledge and experience to effectively run a business. They assume their experience as an engineer, a technician, team leader, or department head is sufficient to ensure business success.

You may be an expert on the products your business sells or the services you offer. But few owners are equally skilled at accounting, human resources, the law, taxes, or any of the other complex and technical areas that comprise running a business. As your business grows, you may find yourself in the Growth Zone with a lack of experience in functional activities that are critical to growth. Lack of experience can cause you to make fatal mistakes that a more experienced entrepreneur would avoid. The key is not to learn it all; the key is to hire the right people to complement your skills.

Effective Management and Leadership

Effective management and leadership skills are essential to business success, and a lack of either can lead to confusion and conflict within the ranks, poor morale and reduced productivity. The most common reason businesses fail is ineffective management. Make it a priority to acquire the skills you need and to strengthen areas where you know you are weak. Your employees look to you for leadership, and it is your responsibility to lead!

Trying to do everything yourself instead of seeking help is a critical mistake. Outsource the activities you do not perform well or have little time to successfully complete. Whether it's hiring new employees or seeking professional help from a lawyer, accountant, or business coach, it's important to know when you're stretched and need help. While paying for help will cost you money, the time saved and knowledge gained will be well worth the investment. You will have peace of mind and be able to focus more on growing your business.

Emotional Intelligence

Daniel Goleman introduced millions of readers to the concept of emotional intelligence (EI) with the publication of his first book on the topic in 1995, *Emotional intelligence*. According to Goleman EI is the amalgamation of psychological skills and traits that he claims accounts for 80% of success in life, not just business. Goleman asserts that skills such as self-awareness and self-motivation are instilled (or destroyed) in childhood, but claims that even adults can learn them and apply them to marriage, business and education.

Since that publication, there has been a surge of research into the biology of intelligence, personality, and emotion. The big idea that initially attracted attention to EI, both within psychology and among the general public is that success in work and life depends on more than just the basic cognitive abilities typically measured by IQ tests and related measures. Success also depends on a number of personal qualities that involve the perception, understanding, and regulation of emotion.

Emotional intelligence (EI) has become one of the hottest buzzwords in corporate America. For instance, when the Harvard Business Review published an article on the topic in 1998, it attracted a higher percentage of readers than any other article published in that periodical in the preceding 40 years. When the CEO of Johnson & Johnson read that article, he was so impressed that he had copies sent out to the 400 top executives in the company worldwide.

Emotional intelligence has been defined as, "The ability to monitor one's own and others' feelings and emotions, to discriminate among them and to use this information to guide one's thinking and actions" (Salovey and Mayer 1990).

Evolutionary Basis

Evolution favored emotions that help us cope with dangerous situations. Emotions evolved because they drive us to take action in the face of danger. We retain the emotional system of our pre-historic ancestors, who regularly faced life-and-death situations. In modern society, those emotions often overwhelmed thought. In a real sense, we have two minds, one that thinks and one that feels. The rational mind lets us think, ponder and reflect. But the emotional mind is impulsive and powerful. Usually, the two work in harmony, but intense feelings sometimes allow the emotional mind to dominate the rational mind.

The brain's emotion centers evolved first. The limbic system which surrounds the brainstem is the center of passionate emotion and also influences learning and memory. Later evolution produced the neocortex where the brain thinks. Meanwhile, on the sides of the brain, there grew the amygdala, a pair of structures that act as a storehouse of emotional memory. The amygdala gives life emotional meaning and passion. In a crisis, it reacts almost instantly, far more quickly than the neocortex. This emotional brain can act independently of the thinking brain. The amygdala gives extra weight to memories of emotional arousal, so we have vivid memories of pleasure or danger.

While the amygdala pushes us to action, the neocortex works like a damper. It stifles or controls feelings. We experience emotional hijackings when the amygdala is triggered, and the neocortex fails to control it. Strong emotions interfere with attention span and every aspect of clear thinking. Your goal should never be to eliminate emotion. Instead, you must find an intelligent balance of reason and emotion.

Components of Emotional Intelligence

IQ contributes only 20% to life success. The rest is the result of emotional intelligence. IQ and emotional intelligence are not opposing competencies. They work separately. It is possible to be intellectually brilliant but emotionally inept. This causes many life problems.

Emotional competencies cluster into groups, each based on a common underlying emotional intelligence capacity. The underlying emotional intelligence capacities are vital if you are to successfully learn the competencies necessary to succeed in business. The five dimensions of emotional intelligence and the 25 emotional competencies are:

Personal Competence	Social Competence
These competencies determine how we manage ourselves.	*These competencies determine how we handle relationships.*
Self-Awareness *Knowing one's internal states, preferences, resources, and intuitions*	**Empathy** Awareness of others' feelings, needs, and concerns
	Understanding others: *Sensing others' feelings and perspectives, and taking an active interest in their concerns*
Emotional awareness: *Recognizing one's emotions and their effects*	
	Developing others: *Sensing others' development needs and bolstering their abilities*
Accurate self-assessment: *Knowing one's strengths and limits*	
Self-confidence: *A strong sense of one's self-worth and capabilities*	**Service orientation:** *Anticipating, recognizing, and meeting customers' needs*
Self-Regulation *Managing one's internal states, impulses, and resources*	**Leveraging diversity:** *Cultivating opportunities through different kinds of people*
Innovation: *Being comfortable with novel ideas, approaches, and new information* **Self-Control:** *Keeping disruptive emotions and impulses in check*	**Political awareness:** *Reading a group's emotional currents and power relationships*
Trustworthiness: *Maintaining standards of honesty and integrity*	**Social Skills** *Adeptness at inducing desirable responses in others*
Conscientiousness: *Taking responsibility for personal performance*	
Adaptability: *Flexibility in handling change*	**Influence:** *Wielding effective tactics for persuasion* **Conflict management:** *Negotiating and resolving disagreements*
Motivation *Emotional tendencies that guide or facilitate reaching goals*	**Communication:** *Listening openly and sending convincing messages*
	Leadership: *Inspiring and guiding individuals and groups*
Achievement drive: *Striving to improve or meet a standard of excellence*	
	Change catalyst: *Initiating or managing change*
Commitment: *Aligning with the goals of the group or organization*	
	Building bonds: *Nurturing instrumental relationships*
Initiative: *Readiness to act on opportunities*	
	Collaboration and cooperation: *Working with others toward shared goals*
Optimism: *Persistence in pursuing goals despite obstacles and setbacks*	**Team capabilities:** *Creating group synergy in pursuing collective goals*

Self-Awareness

It would seem at a glance that our feelings are obvious, but they often are hidden from us. Emotional self-awareness is ongoing attention to one's internal states, including the emotions. It is a neutral state that continues self-examination even during intense emotions. Psychologist John Mayer calls it being "aware of both our mood and our thoughts about that mood." For practical purposes, self-awareness and the ability to change our moods are the same.

Emotions can be and often are unconscious. They begin before a person is consciously aware of the feeling. Unconscious emotions can have a powerful effect on thoughts and reactions, even though we are not aware of them. When we become conscious of them, we can evaluate them. Thus, self-awareness is the foundation for managing emotions and being able to shake off a bad mood.

Self-Regulation

A life without passion would be boring. Our emotional life maintains a constant background hum, rarely becoming intense. Yet managing emotions is a full-time job. Much of what we do, from work to recreation, is an attempt to manage our mood. The art of soothing ourselves is a basic life skill, some say one of the most essential psychic tools. The design of the brain means we have little control over when we will be swept by emotions or what those emotions will be, but we have some control over how long they last.

One of the most difficult emotions to escape is rage, partly because anger is energizing, even exhilarating. It can last for hours and create a hair-trigger state, making people much more easily provoked. When the body is already in an edgy state and something triggers another emotional surge, the ensuing emotion is especially intense.

One way to cool off from anger is to seek distractions. Going off alone helps, as does active exercise, sensual treats, accomplishing some small task, or helping others. One powerful tool is cognitive reframing or looking at your situation in a more positive light.

Self-Motivation

Positive motivation is one key to achievement. The greatest athletes, musicians and chess masters are distinguished by their ability to stick with their arduous practice, year after year, beginning early in life. Emotions determine how we do in life by enhancing or limiting our capacity to use our innate abilities. One critical skill is the ability to restrain emotions and delay impulses, to defer gratification. This is the key to a host of efforts, from dieting to achieving a degree.

Anxiety undermines intellect, while good moods enhance thinking. Those who are adept at harnessing their emotions can use their anxiety for motivation. The relationship between anxiety and performance has been described as an upside-down U. Too little anxiety means no motivation and poor performance. Too much anxiety impairs intellect. Peak performance comes in the middle.

Hope and optimism also play a powerful role in life. Hope means not giving in to negativism or depression in the face of setbacks. Optimism means having a strong expectation that things will turn out all right. Optimists attribute failure to something they can change and therefore do not get depressed about it. Optimism is an emotionally intelligent attitude that boosts performance in the business world. Underlying both hope and optimism is self-efficacy, the belief that one has mastery over the events of one's life and can meet challenges.

Psychologists have identified a peak performance state called flow. This is emotional intelligence at its best. Flow comes when people become fully engaged in a task in which they are highly skilled. Emotions are positive, channeled and directed at the task at hand. It is a state of self-forgetfulness. Full attention is focused on the task. The brain actually becomes calmer and enters a state called flow. The most challenging tasks are finished using minimal energy. Any person can learn flow by repeatedly performing tasks that they love.

Empathy

The more self-aware we are, the more skilled we become at reading the feelings of others. Rapport, the root of caring, arises from the capacity for empathy. Those who can read others' feelings are better adjusted, more popular, outgoing and sensitive. Empathy begins in infancy with the non-verbal physical mirroring between a child and parent. When a child and parent are attuned, the infant is reassured and feels emotionally connected. This requires enough calm to be able to read subtle, non-verbal signals from the other person.

Leadership Style and Emotional Intelligence

Many owners mistakenly assume that leadership style is a function of personality rather than strategic choice. Instead of choosing the one style that suits your temperament, ask which style best addresses the demands of a particular situation. Research has shown that the most successful leaders have strengths in each of the emotional intelligence competencies. There are six basic styles of leadership; each makes use of the key components of emotional intelligence in different combinations. The best leaders don't know just one style of leadership—they're skilled at several and have the flexibility to switch between styles as the circumstances dictate.

Owners often fail to appreciate how profoundly the organizational culture can influence financial results. Studies show that it can account for nearly a third of financial performance. Organizational culture, in turn, is influenced by leadership style. Your style is the way that you motivate employees, gather and use information, make decisions, manage change initiatives, and handle crises. There are six basic leadership styles. Each derives from different emotional intelligence competencies, works best in particular situations, and affects the organizational culture in different ways. Each style of leadership and a brief description are outlined below:

Leadership Style	Coercive	Pacesetting	Authoritative	Affilliative	Democratic	Coaching
The leader's modus operandi	Demands immediate compliance	Sets high standards for performance	Mobilizes people toward a vision	Creates harmony and builds emotional bonds	Forges consensus through participation	Develops people for the future
The style in a phrase	"Do what I tell you.'	"Do as I do, now."	'Come with me.'	'People come first."	"What do you think?"	"Try this.'
Underlying emotional intelligence competencies	Drive to achieve, initiative, self-control	Conscientiousness, drive to achieve, initiative	Self-confidence, empathy, change catalyst	Empathy, building relationships, communication	Collaboration, team leadership, communication	Developing others, empathy, self-awareness
When the style works best	In a crisis, to kick start a turnaround, or with problem employees	To get quick results from a highly motivated and competent team	When changes require a new vision, or when a clear direction is needed	To heal rifts in a team or to motivate people during stressful circumstances	To build buy-in or consensus, or to get input from valuable employees	To help an employee improve performance or develop long-term strengths
Overall impact on culture	Negative	Negative	Most strongly positive	Positive	Positive	Positive

Switching Between Styles

Many studies have shown that the more styles a leader has in her repertoire, the better. Leaders who have mastered four or more styles, especially the authoritative, democratic, affiliative, and coaching styles, have created the most effective culture and business performance.

The most effective leaders switch flexibly among the leadership styles as needed. They don't mechanically match their style to fit a checklist of situations, they are far more fluid. They are sensitive to the impact they are having on others and seamlessly adjust their style to get the best results. These are leaders, for example, who can read in the first minutes of conversation that a talented but underperforming employee has been demoralized by an unsympathetic, do-it-the-way-I-tell-you manager and needs to be inspired through a reminder of why her work matters. Or that leader might choose to re-energize the employee by asking her about her dreams and aspirations and finding ways to make her job more challenging. Or, that initial conversation might signal that the employee needs an ultimatum: improve or leave.

Sarah's Story

Sarah was the general manager of a national food company. She was hired at a time when the business was in a deep crisis. It had not made its profit targets for six years. In the most recent year, it had missed by $5 million. Morale among the management team who were passed over in favor of this "outsider" was miserable; mistrust and resentment were rampant. Sarah's directive from the absentee owner was clear: turn the company around, or I will find someone who will.

From the start, she realized she had a short window to demonstrate effective leadership and to establish rapport and trust. She also knew that she urgently needed to be informed about what was not working, so her first task was to listen to key people.

Her first week on the job she had lunch and dinner meetings with each member of the management team. Sarah sought to get each person's understanding of the current situation. But her focus was not so much on learning how each person diagnosed the problem as on getting to know each manager as a person. Here Sarah employed the affiliative style: she explored their lives, dreams, and aspirations.

She also stepped into the coaching role, looking for ways she could help the team members achieve what they wanted in their careers. For instance, one manager who had been getting feedback that he was a poor team player confided his worries to her. He thought he was a good team member, but he was plagued by persistent complaints. Recognizing that he was a talented executive and a valuable asset to the company, Sarah made an agreement with him to point out (in private) when his actions undermined his goal of being seen as a team player.

She followed the one-on-one conversations with a three-day off-site meeting. Her goal here was team building so that everyone would own whatever solution for the business problems emerged. Her initial stance at the off-site meeting was that of a democratic leader. She encouraged everyone to express freely their frustrations and complaints.

The next day, Sarah had the group focus on solutions: each person made three specific proposals about what needed to be done. As Sarah aggregated the suggestions, a natural consensus emerged about priorities for the business, such as cutting costs. As the group came up with specific action plans, Sarah got the commitment and buy-in she sought.

With that vision in place, Sarah shifted into the authoritative style, assigning accountability for each follow-up step to specific executives and holding them responsible for their accomplishment. For example, the division had been lowering prices on products without increasing its volume. One obvious solution was to raise prices and be certain that the sales team understood value pricing and how to present that when talking with a customer.

Over the following months, Sarah's main stance was authoritative. She continually articulated the group's new vision in a way that reminded each member of how his or her role was crucial to achieving these goals. And, especially during the first few weeks of the plan's implementation, Sarah felt that the urgency of the business crisis justified an occasional shift into the coercive style should someone fail to meet his or her responsibility. After several conversations over the course of several weeks, the sales manager continued to vacillate about implementing the price increase. Sarah replaced him. As she put it, "I had to be brutal about this follow-up and make sure this stuff happened. It was going to take discipline and focus."

As a result of Sarah's leadership style, every aspect of culture improved. People were innovating. They were talking about the company's vision and avowing their commitment to new, clear goals in a documented business plan. The ultimate proof of Sarah's fluid leadership style was both the huge improvement in company culture, and the financial results. The company exceeded its profit target by $5 million.

Key Takeaways

If you have been steadily growing your business, you will need to fill key leadership positions at the appropriate time. Do not make the mistake of taking on all the workload. That will stretch you so thin that you will never be in a position to think strategically, and you will stop growing. As growth really gets going you are going to have to demonstrate your leadership styles. Get to know the styles, and when best to use them.

We all are stuck with whatever innate intelligence we were wired with. But we can learn and grow. One of the best ways to do that is by increasing our emotional intelligence. Unlike innate intelligence, emotional intelligence can be learned and practiced. The sooner you start learning how to nimbly switch from one leadership style to another based on the situation, the faster your business will grow.

The Acceleration Zone $15M to $25M+ of Revenue

CHAPTER 8

Growth Potential

Roadblock #8: My business has great POTENTIAL; I just don't have the energy to grow it.

> "Growth is never by mere chance; it is the result of forces working together."
> -James Cash Penney, Founder of JCPenney

Sustainable Growth

IF YOU ARE like most owners who have entered the Acceleration Zone, you've put a lot of work into your business. You have grown it to over $15M in revenue and you are justifiably proud of your success. You researched your market extensively, and you have an excellent product/market fit. The feedback you get from your customers is fabulous and very rewarding. By all accounts, your business is doing well. The problem is you are stuck.

You're not stuck in bankruptcy, in fact, you're quite profitable. But you thought that by now your company would be one of the ones that broke through to the big time. What's happening? Why can't you get past this point? It's frustrating.

When you look around and see some of your competitors — who

don't offer the same level of customer service, who have an inferior product, who aren't putting in the work you are — and they're breaking through. They're racking up the users or raking in the profits. Why? What is it that they know that you don't? Why is it that they can sustain growth over time and you feel like you're scrambling? What's the secret to sustainable growth?

The Truth About Sustainable Growth

In your mind, you're probably envisioning that illustrious hockey stick of growth, where new customers are on-boarded almost faster than you can handle, and revenues flow freely and fill your coffers. The truth is that except for a tiny, minuscule percentage of companies that have precisely the right combination of luck, timing, and connections, hockey stick growth is not achievable, nor sustainable over the long term. That doesn't mean that you can't enjoy real, sustainable growth. Rather, it means that you need to stop viewing the hockey stick as the model to which you aspire.

What Sustainable Growth Really Looks Like

Real, sustainable growth follows an S-curve. The S shape represents growth over time —it starts out slowly, then picks up speed for rapid growth. But unlike the fabled hockey stick, the S-curve then tapers off as growth slows.

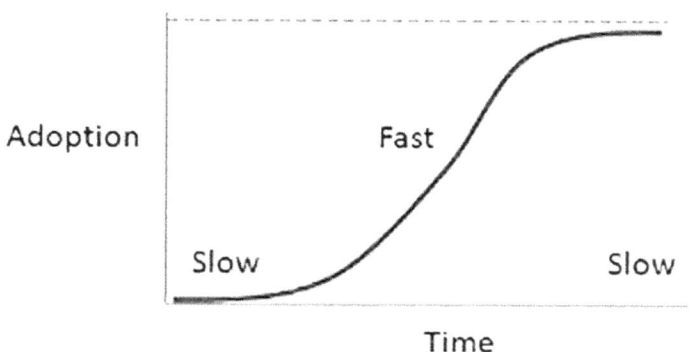

Once you understand what sustainable growth looks like, then you know you don't have to panic when growth begins to slow. Instead, you can recognize that you have reached a significant point on the growth curve known as an inflection point. Inflection points are points where the slope of the curve changes significantly. All companies that experience growth will encounter strategic inflection points. The key is to recognize this as a critical point when you need to take action to continue to grow. A fundamental shift is necessary.

Organic Growth

When you started your business, you focused on growing your customer base, reinvesting profits in new assets for greater income, and improving productivity to increase your bottom line. Long-term organic growth requires effective management, effective planning, and a deep understanding of the customers and industries being served.

The dependency on internal resources can be viewed as either a benefit or drawback. Using only internal resources means your company will probably grow slowly and incrementally, which can allow it to quickly navigate through different market cycles and turns. Organic growth is usually the preferred strategy of businesses that are comfortable with a more controlled progression and currently have a small share of the market.

Inorganic Growth

Inorganic growth focuses on achieving expansion through mergers or acquisitions. One of the key benefits of this strategy is its ability to deliver very substantial changes to a business in a very short amount of time. Most often, inorganic growth is pursued by businesses looking for new employees, new products, or new markets. A smart, well-executed merger or acquisition can help achieve each of these goals, or all three simultaneously.

The inorganic strategy often makes sense for near-retirement business owners that are looking to maximize the value of their business before a sale. If a business owner is planning to sell in five years, a well-positioned acquisition might boost revenues and market position, yielding a significantly higher valuation from an investor. Pursuing a merger or acquisition will entail some risk, primarily the business expanding too quickly, loss of focus, or cultural integration issues, but can be very successful with proper preparation and post-merger integration.

Benefits of Using an Acquisition Strategy for Growth

- At times the most effective way to remove a competitor from the marketplace is by acquiring them.
- Acquiring a competitor in order to gain functional expertise or access to new products and new markets can open up new opportunities.
- As your business grows, you will be better positioned to attract top-quality employees by offering competitive pay, and benefits.
- Small companies merged into a larger entity may qualify for low-interest bank financing to fuel further organic growth or additional acquisitions.
- With each acquisition that you make you can benefit from increased prestige and visibility. You will have the opportunity to benefit from PR releases to grow awareness in your markets. The end result is the ability to create a lasting and valuable brand identification that can accelerate sales in a regional market.
- As your business grows, you will be better positioned to take on the risk of entering new markets with new products, increasing your growth possibilities.

Why business growth is important

Growth means a lot of things to different people. I am referring to the kind of growth that allows you to grow as a person and as a leader, grows your team, grows your business capability, and grows both your revenue and earnings. It grows a wealth that is far more satisfying than money alone. There's nothing wrong with being a permanently small business. But if you want to remain small, recognize the risks you assume if you remain small.

What happens when you do NOT grow?

In Ch 2 I discussed what can happen if you become complacent. When you fall into a complacency trap, you put your financial future in jeopardy and you risk the following:

- Your earnings will stay about the same if they don't shrink
- You won't be able to help your customers with innovative products and services
- You will limit the potential of your employees
- You won't be able to pay your employees more
- You won't create additional jobs
- You won't be able to provide more for the families of people in your organization
- You'll lose great employees who want to grow
- Your competition will grow
- You might be left behind in your industry
- You may get bored in the business

No business stays the same. It either gets bigger or smaller. Better or worse. You either grow or you shrink. But that doesn't mean you should grow simply for the sake of growth. One great reason to grow is to give your employees the opportunity to grow and flourish. Grow for the opportunities and "wealth" you are creating for yourself and for your employees. When your employees have opportunities, they are more likely to become engaged, and I discussed the importance of that in Chapter 3.

Every Inflection Point Offers an Opportunity Growth

You know you're at a strategic inflection point when growth begins to slow significantly, stops, or even reverses. That inflection point is a significant moment in the life cycle of your company. But if you recognize the inflection point for what it is, you can navigate it successfully. Unfortunately, there's no single solution you can use to navigate every inflection point effectively. But if you adapt and innovate each time you reach such a point you can continue to be successful.

In some cases, navigating an inflection point means innovating a change in your product to realign your offering with your target market. Other times, you may need to make improvements to the processes within your marketing funnel. Or, you might need to invent something entirely new to meet the needs of your ideal customer.

Regardless of the size of your company, if it is built on the foundation of the growth framework, and if your people are grounded in a growth mindset and have access to the right training and education, you should be able to navigate these inflection points successfully. Approach each inflection point as an opportunity to transform your company into a competitive powerhouse by creating a customer-centric culture and encouraging collaboration between your various teams (marketing, technology, product development, sales, etc.).

Be Aware of External Factors that Threaten Sustainable Growth

Sometimes a revenue stall is related to external factors. When this happens, you cannot ignore the evidence in front of you. You can't refuse to see what's happening in the world as having an impact on your business. You can't block out external factors and plunge ahead as if nothing has changed. How you respond to external factors depends on what exactly those factors are. What's critical is that you act strategically, based on the knowledge that you are facing an inflection point.

Identify Internal Threats to Sustainable Growth

When the threat to sustainable growth comes from within your company, it can be difficult to identify. If you have fallen into a complacency trap, you may not recognize that you have pulled your employees into the trap with you. Getting yourself out of the trap and pulling your employees out can be a traumatic experience for all involved.

In this situation, you need buy-in before you can enact change. You cannot simply issue a mandate and expect everyone in the company to suddenly be on board because you said so. Instead, you will need to put in the time and team training to help your employees understand the underlying need for the change, and give them the skill sets they will need to be an active part of the change.

You may discover that some of your employees simply cannot get on board. You have some tough decisions to make. Employees who are not growth-minded will not be able to contribute effectively, and may even actively work to disrupt change.

Create a Frictionless Experience to Drive Sustainable Growth

When you want to improve growth and retain the customers you already have, you must ensure that your entire marketing funnel, from attracting potential customers through onboarding and all the way through turning customers into advocates is frictionless. Make it easy. The entire customer experience must be nothing short of pure bliss. Hide the complexities. And once you have those customers, hold them closely. For more on this see Chapter 6.

Nurture your niche

Chasing "bad" revenue by offering a wide array of products and services is common among growth companies. The easiest way to grow is to sell more things to your existing customers, so the temptation is to continually add adjacent product and service lines. The problem that can arise from this is that each new product line extension misses the mark slightly for your ideal customer. You begin to widen the definition of your ideal customer, and the result can be that your ideal customers no longer find you relevant. When they believe you have abandoned them, they will abandon you and migrate to those companies that speak directly to them. When this happens, growth will not only halt, you could reverse course.

Growth vs. Value: not all revenue is created equally

Growth requires a qualitative and quantitative understanding of metrics to allocate resources, the willingness to accept slower short-term rates to realize faster ones down the road, and a daily, laser-like focus on performance.

When you look ahead to next year, will your growth come from selling more to your existing customers or finding new customers for your existing products and services? The answer may have a profound impact on the value of your business.

Focusing on your niche is one of many areas where the long-term value of your business is at odds with short-term profit. For example, if you wanted to maximize your short-term profit, you might avoid investing in new technology or hiring a sales manager, arguing that both investments would hinder short-term profit. A company that builds enduring value finds a way to deliver profit in the short term while simultaneously focusing its strategy on what increases the value of the business.

Ansoff Matrix

To brainstorm how to grow beyond the niche that got you started, consider the Ansoff Matrix. It was first published in the Harvard Business Review in 1957 but remains a helpful framework for business owners today.

Sometimes called the Product/Market Expansion Grid, the Ansoff Matrix shows four ways that businesses can grow, and it can help you think through the risks associated with each option.

		Medium Risk New Products	High Risk Diversification
Markets/Customers	**New**	Low Risk Increase Market Share	Medium Risk Market Develolpment
	Existing	Existing	New
		Products and Services	

Existing Products to Existing Customers

It's natural to feel like you're being greedy when you go back to the same customers for more of their dollars, but the opposite can often be true. Your best customers are usually the ones who know and like you the most and are often pleased to find out that you – someone they trust – are offering something they need.

If you want to sell more of your existing products to your existing customers, draw up a simple chart of your products and services. Don't be afraid to dust off those old products to which you haven't paid much attention lately. List your best customers' names down one side of the paper and your products across the top. Then cross-reference your customer list with your product list to identify opportunities to sell your best customers more of your existing products.

Market Penetration

The existing products to existing customers approach can be expanded to a more generic strategy called market penetration, selling more products or services to established customers, or by attracting new customers within your existing market segments. This is the least risky strategy because it leverages your existing resources and capabilities, and your existing knowledge of the market segments. A market penetration strategy is an appropriate growth strategy and should be explored thoroughly when you make the conscious decision to grow your business.

In a growing market, simply maintaining market share will result in growth, and there may be opportunities to increase market share if competitors reach capacity limits. But, to ensure success despite weakness in the economy, changes in tax and tariff rates and other external factors you must set goals, develop plans, and execute those plans.

Common routes to accomplishing this strategy include:

- Increase in promotion and distribution
- Increase brand recognition and image
- Price decrease to gain market share
- Acquisition of a rival in the same market
- Drive out your competitors
- Dominate growth markets
- Improve customer experience
- Modest product refinements
- Increase usage: "Supersize it, you want fries with that?"
- New occasions: "Beer, it's not just for breakfast anymore!"
- Create new uses "Baking soda in the refrigerator."
- Shorten replacement cycle "Toothbrushes with a color change."

One key constraint is that you cannot allow anything in your drive to grow market share to compromise your existing success. You need to be aware of what has made your products a success so far and ensure that nothing you do will undermine that success.

You should give this strategy careful consideration if you are not in a position to invest heavily or are not comfortable taking risks, as the amount of risk associated with this strategy is relatively low. It relies on you having successful products in a market that you already know well. However, market penetration has limits, and once the market approaches saturation, another strategy must be pursued if the firm is to continue to grow.

Market Penetration tactics

Price adjustment

The tactic of Price Adjustment is one of the most widely used market penetration tactics. Use it judiciously as overdoing it can lead to adverse results. Increasing, or more typically, lowering your product pricing may result in share increase but the effect of this tactic can be temporary as competitors may drop their price to avoid losing market share. This can set off a death spiral of price cuts which will be difficult to survive unless you are the low-cost provider. Price changes may also affect your brand image and positioning.

Increase promotions

Another tactic for market penetration strategy is to increase the promotions for your product and thereby increase pull from customers. By giving trade discounts, sales promotion discounts, and other benefits to the customers you may penetrate the market more quickly. The most common type of sales promotions is consumer discounts.

Premiumization

Increasing your selling prices by improving quality or perceived quality using branding techniques.

Share of Wallet

Selling more to your existing customers as opposed to looking for new customers.

Increase reach

If your product is channel driven, then increasing the reach of your product is a tactic you should consider. The way to do this is to find more channel dealers and channel partners. The trick here is to keep the channel partner motivated at all times to do business with you. By increasing reach, and having your products everywhere through channel dealers and retailers, you ensure that your customers can get your product wherever she goes.

Increase usage

By increasing the usage of a product, you can increase its consumption thereby penetrating the market even further.

Attract competition's customers and dealers

By dropping your price to a distributor in a specific area you can increase your market penetration by decreasing the number of products sold by competitors.

Non-users to start the product

Encouraging non-users to start using the product is a tough task, and this is where marketing is key.

Market Development

A market development strategy involves selling your existing product/service line into new target markets. The development of new markets for your core products may be a good strategy if your company's core competencies are related more to its products than to its experience with a specific market segment.

Because the firm is expanding into a new market, a market development strategy typically has more risk than a market penetration strategy. A thorough analysis should be conducted to ensure there is truly a good market/product fit.

Customer segmentation should be conducted considering the following different ways to segment the market:

- Demographic segments
  Characteristics of a population including race, ethnicity, gender, age, education, profession, occupation, income level, and marital status.

- Geographic segments
  Promoting the product in geographic areas that were not previously supported

- Psychographic segments
  Dividing a market into different segments based on consumers' personality traits, values, interests, or lifestyles.

This strategy is more likely to be successful when:

- Your company has a unique technology it can leverage in the new market
- It benefits from economies of scale as it increases output
- There is a good market/product fit, or the product can be modified slightly to better meet the needs of a specific segment

Product Development

A product development strategy may be appropriate if your company's strengths are related to its specific customers or the value chain in general rather than to the specific products you sell. Product development allows you to leverage your strengths in a market segment by developing a new product for that segment.

The duration and expense of the development can be a relatively modest expenditure of time and money if the current product can be relatively easily modified and the current production process can be used to produce the new product. However, it can be a very large expense if the product is a significant change to the current products or new equipment and additional processing steps are required. For these reasons, the strategy carries significantly more risk than simply attempting to leverage your current technology in new markets. It is not only risky; no level of success is assured. To increase your odds of success review Chapter 4 where I discussed new product development from a management perspective.

A strategy of product development is particularly suitable when product differentiation can result in a sustainable competitive advantage. You will need:

- Research & development capability
- Detailed insights into customer needs (and how they change)
- Market Orientation
- New Product Development Strategies
- New Product Development Process
- New Product Development Teams
- Technology

Diversification

The last strategy is Diversification. This growth strategy involves selling new products into new markets. It is the riskiest strategy because it involves risk associated with developing the product, and risk due to a lack of experience in the new market segment. Before pursuing a diversification strategy understand these risks and potential rewards. Risk increases if you cannot leverage your core competencies in product development, or if the markets you are pursuing require new channels and new promotion.

An advantage of diversification is that it helps to spread the risk associated with downturns in any one product line, or market segment. Diversification can be achieved through one of three strategies.

Horizontal diversification

You may be able to expand your product portfolio with an item that is similar to an existing product. This has the advantage that your company already has expertise in manufacturing technology, and you can leverage your existing processes. The new products speak to new customer groups as well as those who've bought from you in the past. Compared to other diversification measures, horizontal diversification is the lower risk.

Vertical diversification

Vertical diversification is less about expanding the product range than about expanding your control over the value chain. For example, you can take over the distribution of your goods yourself (forward integration) or take further steps in the manufacturing process into your own hands (backward integration). This makes you less dependent on suppliers or dealers. The additional services can also be resold to other customers. Setting up new production facilities may require a considerable investment which leads to an increased risk.

Lateral diversification

You take the greatest risk with lateral diversification: instead of concentrating on your existing business and expanding it; you go in a completely new direction. With a completely different product, you are placing yourself in a completely new market in which you have no expertise. This approach is associated with high costs and success is certainly not guaranteed. This is why lateral diversification is only recommended if you have the financial strength to survive a complete failure.

Analysis Paralysis

Some schools of thought believe that the use of strategic management tools such as the Ansoff Matrix can result in an overuse of analysis. In fact, Ansoff himself thought about this and it was he who first mentioned the now-famous phrase "paralysis by analysis". Make sure that you do not fall victim to procrastination caused by excessive planning.

Sue's Story

Things had really taken off in Sue's marketing business. She was landing new clients regularly, referrals were coming in, and her revenue was increasing every year. She now led a team of 16 talented young employees to engage the growing client base.

As the business grew, the scope of engagements was all over the place. Production problems were at an all-time high. Everyone was getting burned out, juggling too many things, and working long days.

Sue had not been able to take a vacation since she started the business. She couldn't afford to bring on more talent to help with the extra workload, and she knew she couldn't put it all on the young team she had. Sue feared that her two key employees were looking to leave the agency just to find some sanity. On top of those problems, while the top-line revenue was increasing, overall profit margins were declining.

She began to put in longer and longer days; twelve hours at the office had become the norm, six, even seven days a week. With each new client, the workload increased, and she finally realized she could not continue on the path of insanity.

Clearly what had worked to get the agency to this level was not working at the size it had become. There was chaos everywhere. The idea of taking on a new client brought feelings of fear and dread, instead of the exhilaration and excitement that had been there before. The team was not performing as it should have been and the agency simply had no ability to grow beyond its current level.

She decided to get help, and I got involved.

Mapping the process

We conducted a mapping of the people, product, and processes. We found issues with business processes, business systems, and a lack of strategic direction that led to confusion and uncontrolled growth. These issues led to declining margins. Several areas within the agency were contributing to the problem and that meant the solutions needed to touch all aspects of the business.

We were able to:

- Identify the clients that provided the largest opportunity for growth and profits.

- Uncover bad-fit clients that were costing the agency more than the revenue they brought in
- Internal team roles that were underutilized or had the potential for expansion
- Internal team roles that were redundant and the resources could be redeployed
- Lack of some processes to fully meet organizational needs

By going through a strategic planning process Sue realized that not all revenue is good revenue. She pared down the breadth of products/services the company offered and turned away clients who were not a good fit with their capabilities.

Over a period of 8 months, new business processes were introduced, and productive ways of working replaced ineffective ones. A solid foundation was laid with each new business process implementation.

Results

Costly clients were let go. More profitable clients were added to the books. Processes and procedures were implemented to manage work. Staffing decisions were made to improve service. Team members have ownership and empowerment in their roles. What was a 16-person agency that was barely profitable is now a thriving 31-person agency that knows how to scale.

Sue now has the tools and confidence to continue to grow her business. Best of all, she was able to cut back her hours to about 40/week and took a one-week vacation for the first time since she started the business. One of her goals is to take a 2-week vacation in Hawaii next spring.

Key Takeaways

Here are five questions I suggest you discuss with your team:

1. Why do we lose business?

2. Who are our most profitable customers?

3. Are any of our value propositions interchangeable with our competitors?

4. Should we be offering more, or less, choice in our product portfolio?

5. What potential sales partnerships and industry alliances should we be planning for in our future?

You might assume your people are thinking about these questions. The reality is that these questions are often put on the back burner due to the pressures of daily business. Asking these questions at your staff meetings has the potential to not only change the trajectory of your company but also to make your meetings more engaging and aligning. Growth focused companies outperform operationally focused companies, so if you want to be successful, focus on growth.

CHAPTER 9

Scalability

Roadblock #9: We are a small business, I can't grow like Amazon.

> "Only those who will risk going too far can possibly find out how far one can go." – T.S. Eliot

What is Scalability and how does that differ from Growth

GROWTH MAY TAKE place in any number of methods as discussed in Chapter 8 including increasing revenue by increasing market share, developing new products or services, entering new markets, or any combination thereof. The methods for achieving growth may be organic or inorganic. Each of these strategies can result in additional capital that can be used to acquire new customers for existing or new value propositions. But, if you want to do more than simply grow your existing business, if you want to be hugely successful and make a big impact, then you must consider the scalability of your business model. Whether you are starting a new business, or looking to take your existing business to the next level, scalability is an important factor to consider.

Growing versus scaling

A typical business that is growing adds resources at about the same rate as its revenue growth. If it is currently operating at a 20% profit margin, and it increases revenue by $1M, the profit earned on that additional $1M of revenue is $200K. The other $800K is additional expenses. A scalable company, however, adds revenue at an exponential rate while adding resources at a much lower rate. Its profit margin increases dramatically as its revenue increases. A company that is scalable adds $1M in revenue and increases its profit by $900K or more. Only $100K of additional expenses are needed to support the revenue increase.

Scalability Perspectives

Scalable growth is built on an organizational foundation that can scale with the growth. It has systems, processes, and standardized practices to resolve the productivity, communication, and management issues that crop up as your business grows. Scalable growth can only be achieved by a business that has been built for scale.

The most dominant companies to emerge from the past 2 decade's tech boom have proven that huge and healthy growth is all about scaling. By adopting a scalable business model, these firms have generated huge profits without all the budgetary strains that plague traditional growth models. A replicable system for delivering a product (whatever that may be, from services to technology) allows businesses to increase their customer base without increasing their overhead at the same rate. A scalable business model delivers consistent growth and increasing margin over time.

Software companies offer a strong example: once the development stage is complete, they can infinitely replicate their end product and sell it to customers at little or no additional cost to the business. The more efficient the mechanism for mass production, the more scalable your company is. WhatsApp is a prime example of a successfully scaled business. The WhatsApp business model drove quickly adding customers while requiring few additional resources. When Facebook announced it had bought the company for $16B it had only 55 employees, but over 450M active customers.

By contrast, the traditional growth model fosters a vicious cycle of inefficiency–a company gains a few new clients, so they hire more people to service those clients, adding costs at nearly the same rate that they're adding revenue.

Scalable workforce

A scalable business has a workflow that allows for expansion and contraction. A company that anticipates rapid growth needs workflow solutions that will work just as well for a team of 50 as they do for the initial team of five. A company that expands operations quickly for the holiday shopping season and then scales back down after the holiday rush is over, requires scalability upward *and* downward, with minimal impact on operational costs.

Maintain Consistency and Quality

Scalability is what ensures that your company can produce consistently excellent products and services as it grows, with a minimum of growing pains. Scalability is about capacity and capability. When your company's workflows are scalable, you have an enormous advantage over companies that are not built to scale. It requires planning, some funding, and the right systems, staff, processes, technology, and partners.

If growth causes your company to stumble because of confusion, orders going unfulfilled, insufficient staff, miscommunication, insufficient manufacturing capacity or delivery capacity –you're going to have unhappy customers. And unhappy customers will stop you dead in your tracks.

How scalable is your business?

Think about scalability as a spectrum, not a binary choice. No business is 100% scalable or non-scalable. You may have chosen a business model that is very low on the scalability spectrum, but that does not mean you are stuck with that model forever. The key is to think differently about your business model.

A bespoke hat maker, for example, is low on the spectrum because every head is a different shape and must be measured precisely, she may have an abundance of hair or a complete lack of it, he will want a specific style and will want it adorned with specific flourishes. All of this customization must be handled by a highly skilled individual, whose time limits how many customers can be served. All these considerations mean this business is very low on scalability.

However, if you have this type of business, you may be able to employ a different business model that allows you to make your business much more scalable. To do that, you must identify aspects of your value proposition that can be replicated quickly with little additional resources (costs or time). It is important to distinguish these areas before you begin to grow, rather than finding out that a process is broken once you have hundreds or thousands of disgruntled customers giving you one star on their favorite hater list.

I have found that the owners of service businesses find it difficult to see how to scale their service business. So, while the comments below are fairly general, and are applicable to all businesses, I have made them with a service business in mind.

Your Target Market/ Ideal Customer

Everything you do should be for the benefit of your ideal customer. If you want to make your business more scalable, you might need to tweak your target market. For most business owners this usually means narrowing down your focus to a smaller target market/niche in which you can specialize and own the market. Trying to be all things to all people may be a recipe for survival, but not for growth.

For example, trying to teach marketing strategies to anyone who has a pulse and money to spend is hard to market. Teaching a subset of marketing skills, for example, referral strategies are much easier to market. And if you dig down a little more, teaching referral strategies to financial advisors is even more scalable. To scale, you have to find a group of people who identify with the problems you can solve and then become a hero to them. Nurture your niche.

Creating Scalable Processes

In order to scale any business, you need to develop standardized business processes that are designed to handle high volumes of customers, with few resources. Consider the following avenues to create a more scalable business.

Automate wherever possible

To improve efficiency and standardization, you'll next want to look for areas that can be automated. That includes not only your key service functions but also your marketing functions. You can't scale unless you have a huge demand, and that means that many people need to know about you. Word-of-mouth advertising is not scalable, and neither is direct marketing.

Content marketing, on the other hand, is one of the most scalable growth methods. Content marketing has evergreen value and viral potential, making it the marketing method of choice for most scaling businesses.

Document the Process

If your process is going to be scalable, you need it to be documented to a point where any person assigned to a task can quickly and easily get it done. It needs to be detailed to a point where a new intern could do it without having to ask questions.

Onboarding Standardization

Consistency is imperative to the success of any business. You want to make sure that each customer receives the same time, attention, and quality of work. This is particularly important during the onboarding phase since an in-depth discovery process is key to a strong relationship. Having a centralized onboarding process makes training easier, allows everyone on the onboarding team to understand the limits of customization, and ensures a consistent experience across all customers.

Core Function Standardization

Scalability must focus on your company's core functions. By standardizing your company's core functions, you'll begin to build the foundation for long-term success, rather than operating on reactive, short-term fixes. Do what you are good at and sell that to those who have value for your products/services. Think carefully and choose deliberately before offering new services that are outside of your core competencies. While this can result in growth, it may not result in scalability. Customization is one of the reasons why most businesses will never scale. Nurture your niche and focus on your ideal customer.

Project Management

Excellent project management is an essential component of scalability. As your business grows, you'll have more and more work to manage. Each client will become a new project, and each project will probably have sub-projects. Create a roadmap of project management from the very beginning so your workflow won't be impeded by oncoming growth. If everyone follows the roadmap, every customer arrives at the same place.

Checklists

Checklists will help ensure defined company standards are applied to each interaction your team has with clients. There should be a customized checklist for each client, which is built using your company's standard practices.

Overall Service Management

No matter what industry you're in, if you're a service business, service is what you're selling. That means you need to put measures in place to manage it. When it comes to service management, you must have a team approach to solving clients' problems. Getting buy-in from other team members, or from other teams, can enhance clients' experiences and reinforce consistency across your business.

Defining Service Standards

As a service-oriented business, you need to have service standards that are well defined with clear expectations for both your staff and your customers. These standards should be ingrained in your company culture.

Service Rules.

Define your organization's service rules so everyone is on the same page when urgent situations arise, ensuring there are procedures and policies that everyone must follow. Most service businesses do a good job developing best practices for standard services. Unfortunately, exceptions will occur, and an ill-prepared team without procedures in place for those exceptions may perform poorly in the face of unexpected surprises.

Response Time

Every client should expect a response to an inquiry within a specific time window.

Train the Client Liaisons

As a service provider, you're an extension of your clients' teams. You want to be on the same page with your liaisons, so take advantage of every training opportunity to help your client partner get acquainted with your processes. By helping liaisons understand their roles, and giving them the support they need to be successful as a liaison, you're helping to achieve success for both your own company and your client.

Productize Your Service

Scaling up a service business is difficult because it does not have the benefits of being a tangible product. Treating your services as products by bundling them into packages is a great way to scale up. Review the types of services customers have requested or services that complement your current offerings and then bundle them together into a package. You may find that you can offer the bundle at a lower price versus selling each service individually while increasing revenue and earnings substantially. The key is to adapt your business model so one bundle can be sold multiple times, instead of only once per client.

Pricing

A productized service is sold as a "package" for a set price. Pricing is based on market factors and value of the item being sold, versus an hourly rate plus profit margin tacked on. Products aren't sold based on custom quotes. Think of an e-commerce site or retail store. The price of an item is clearly marked. Readily available pricing will be crucial if you want to scale from a single sale into thousands of sales. Doing custom quotes is usually time-consuming and keeps you from growing.

Clearly Define the Offerings

To make a profit selling a service like it's a product (and avoid scope creep, which can eat up profits), it helps to clearly define what the customer gets with each price level.

Recurring Revenue

A productized service business may be presented as a subscription. Think of your online accounting software or online help desk system. Instead of a one-time purchase of software, you may get a hosted solution that you access online and pay a monthly fee to use. If you look for them, you may find a number of recurring revenue models that can be built into your business. Examples of recurring revenue models include:

- The Network Model

- The Surprise Box Model
- The Library Model
- The Private Club Model
- The front of the Line Model
- The Membership Model
- The Simplifier Model
- The Consumables Model
- The Peace of Mind Model
- Software as a Service

Change Your Business Model

If you want to achieve scalability, but you are using a business model that is not scalable, you have two choices. You can work 168 hours per week, or you can change your business model. Consider how to change your thinking so that you have a business model that can be scaled.

Identify potential strategic partners.

Scalability typically involves connecting strategic partners to the value proposition, either through sharing activities or resources. Are there potential strategic partners that could perform activities in your business model, or provide resources to it, in ways that would help improve the value proposition to your customers?

Leverage assets owned by others

If you look at the business model of many service-based businesses like Uber, Lyft, and Airbnb you will see that they are leveraging other people's assets. For example, Uber does not own many cars and Airbnb does not own much real estate. These companies have figured out how to take underutilized assets and connect them with users of the assets through software. These companies were able to scale so quickly relative to older companies because they did not have to worry about having the capital or resources to acquire these assets.

A Road Map for Scalability

Asking the right questions can trigger ideas about how to re-configure a business model. You need to explore novel ways of doing business and that means analyzing how the new business model would play out for your company. Consider the following questions:

- How can you challenge your existing way of thinking about the business?
- What would you need to do differently to implement this business model?
- Which other companies excel at what you are trying to do, and what can you learn from them?
- What are the key value drivers of your current business model and proposed models?
- Could this business model lead to scalability?
- Are there potential strategic partners that can offer features, at minimal or no cost to your business, that enrich the existing value proposition to your customers, while receiving value themselves?
- Are there alternative configurations that free your business model from existing capacity constraints?
- Would it make sense to establish a platform for other businesses to buy into and thus create alternative ways of generating revenue?
- Is it possible to change the role of existing stakeholders and utilize them in multiple roles in the business model?
- Who would pay for either access to your customer base or knowledge about your customers and their characteristics?
- Which mechanisms are in place to create customer lock-in?
- How agile is your company in reacting to threats from new entrants or new technologies?

Analyze the scalability attributes of business model options

Analyze the attributes of the various options and consider how they might be configured to achieve accelerating returns on investments.

Scalability Finder

To start the process of finding a scalable model, I suggest using a simple 4X4 matrix to determine which services you currently provide are capable of being scaled.

To effectively scale your business the products/services you offer must be both highly differentiated, and also very teachable. Look at every service you offer and plot it on this chart. If your offerings are similar to your competitors, they are more of a commodity than a highly differentiated offering. And, if that offering requires highly trained and skilled personnel to effectively deliver the service, you probably have an offering that is not teachable. The key is to find those products/services that are valuable to your customers, highly differentiated and can be delivered without human interaction, or by an employee with a modest amount of training.

The benefits of differentiation are huge for a service-based business including:

- You do not have to compete on price alone.
- Since you have distinguished yourself from your competitors, the prospective client cannot reduce their choice to the dimension of cost alone.
- You have a greater appeal to your target audience.
- Since you are different (and, presumably, better), you become a more appealing choice. This makes it easier to generate interest and close sales.
- There is no direct substitute.
- If you are demonstrably different from your competitors, you cannot be directly compared to them. Instead, prospects have to focus on the qualitative value of your difference. This adds value that other options lack.
- You increase loyalty.
- The combination of greater value and the lack of comparable substitutes can generate greater loyalty to your firm. There is no good reason to switch (if you are delivering on your promise) and no comparable alternative to switch to.
- You can command higher fees.
- If your differentiation adds true value and is not available elsewhere, you should be able to command higher fees. This is especially true if your differentiator is based on specialized expertise.

This matrix can be expanded to a dozen attributes if you want to get more granular, but the above matrix is a good starting point. Once you find the offerings that have the highest potential for scalability, search for ways these can be automated, or turned over to low skill employees.

Stephen's Story

Taking a startup from creation to a sustainable, scalable, profitable business model is a rare and special endeavor. Founded in 2000 by Stephen Kaufer and Langley Steinert, Boston-based TripAdvisor is a travel website that provides reviews and other information for consumers about travel destinations around the world. The company is now pervasive, with 390 million unique visitors each month scouring the site for reviews of hotels, restaurants, and sites around the globe.

The company started with a very different business model in mind. In founding TripAdvisor in 2000, Kaufer wanted to take his hard-core engineering skills and apply them to vertical search in travel. That is, build a massive database of travel information that provided a white label search engine for travel sites like Expedia and Travelocity.

Kaufer raised $4M in venture capital funding, and after a year and a half, he had no clients, no revenue, and was running out of money. Then, 9/11 hit and the travel industry was decimated.

Fortunately, the company had built up TripAdvisor.com as a demo site to show prospective clients what a vertical search engine could do. When he saw TripAdvisor.com start to pick up traffic, he decided to pursue an online advertising-based business model with banner ads. "Going B2C was daunting and not in our core DNA," Kaufer remarked. But testing hypotheses was very much in the company's DNA, as well as evaluating data to learn and adjust. TripAdvisor, in effect, was a model lean start-up with an engineering-driven, product-focused founder.

After a few weeks of watching no click-throughs, Kaufer executed his second pivot: a cost per click model (now known as CPC). Every time a consumer clicked on a hotel to book a room, TripAdvisor would charge the hotel something. Suddenly, everything changed. Three months into launching the new model, TripAdvisor was earning $70K per month and achieved breakeven. The company has grown profitably ever since. Kaufer originally hired editors to comb the Web for great travel articles and link to them and then allowed users to post their own reviews on the site as a whim. When the company saw that user reviews got all the traffic, they adjusted to focus on user reviews, such that fresh, authentic content was always available and didn't cost the company any money to produce.

With these adjustments, TripAdvisor grew rapidly and successfully. The company agreed to be acquired by Expedia/IAC in 2003 for $210 million in cash, a huge win for all, particularly given their amazing capital efficiency. Under Expedia, TripAdvisor continued to flourish and grow. It would feature Expedia's ads on their site and reap the revenue benefit when users clicked on those ads. Expedia grew to account for roughly one-third of the company's revenues. In December 2011, Expedia felt it wasn't getting full economic credit for TripAdvisor buried within its financials and so spun TripAdvisor out as an independent company, where it now trades on the NASDAQ with a $6.5 billion market capitalization as of this writing.

Focus on Finding A Great Business Model

After some searching, TripAdvisor found a magical business model, representing social media and user-generated content at its best. Content is free and supplied by consumers who write reviews voluntarily. These consumers allow this content and their own engagement to be monetized without asking for anything in return. Customer acquisition is driven mainly through Search Engine Optimization, thanks to the huge volume of great content. Advertisers are brought to the site and driven mainly through self-service channels, so there is no need for a large sales force or account management team. As a result, gross margins are a phenomenally high 98% and EBITDA margins are 47%.

Network Model

TripAdvisor is a classic example of a network effect business and a reminder of how financially attractive network effect businesses can become at scale. There are three sides to the network: the consumer, the venue and the advertiser. The network becomes more valuable as it grows to each party--with more consumers providing more interesting content, more venues providing more access to vacation options and more advertisers offering deals and convenient bookings.

Maintain a Sense of Urgency

Kaufer's description of the TripAdvisor culture and development process makes it clear that he has been able to maintain a strong sense of urgency, even at scale. "No matter how large we are, I always want to maintain a startup mentality," said Kaufer.

Maintain a Product-Focused Culture

Kaufer described that the company culture encouraged testing and learning. "I enjoy focusing on building a great product," he commented simply. "I can maintain that focus as we grow because I have a fantastic executive team who enjoys doing things that I don't enjoy doing."

Key Takeaways

If you want to scale your business, you must first have a holistic view of your business and know where you want to take it. Look at your offerings and determine if you have a scalable business model, or if you need to change your model.

Always focus on your ideal customer. Develop offerings focused on your ideal customer and do not be tempted to move your target to adjacent markets. Nurture your niche.

You will need to predict the kind of challenges your business might face in its journey towards the kind of growth you wish to achieve. Find solutions that will address these challenges. Scale-up, once you know your business is ready to meet every challenge it can encounter.

CHAPTER 10

Who Needs a Coach?

Roadblock #10: I don't need any outside advice, I've got it covered.

> "It's what you learn after you know it all,
> that counts." - John Wooden

THIS WAS THE year you decided to make a breakthrough. You set goals, laid out some plans, and assigned key people to execute the plans. The first quarter was off to a great start. The sales group was doing a great job. Orders were coming in fast and furious. You felt very good about achieving your goals. As the quarter ended you were on track to have a record year.

First Quarter Review

When your accountant called to schedule your quarterly review, you detected a note of concern in her voice, but you brushed it off. After all, she had just finished the bulk of her tax work, and she typically worked 60 to 70 hours a week from January to April. She was probably just tired, and for good reason. The two of you got together the next week, and she presented you with some disturbing reports.

While quarterly revenue was up almost 15% year over year, earnings were down slightly. How could that be you asked?

She pointed out that you had hired an additional salesperson to generate the revenue so your overhead increased. COGS was up, your gross margin was down, Operations and overhead were up, and the net result was a drop in earnings. The two of you discussed the problems and how to improve the situation. While your accountant was good at finding the issues, the only advice she had was that you need to fix those problems.

When you dug into the situation a little more you realized that Operations was having trouble keeping up with the volume of orders, and QC was rejecting more product than normal. The rejections and rework were costing a bundle. The Operations group was working overtime to keep up with orders so Operations costs were up. You instructed your operations manager to fix the situation.

But you know in your heart that isn't going to solve your problems, they go deeper than that, and you do not know what to do. It's not your fault. But it is your responsibility to fix it. So, you have a couple of choices:

- Get a master's degree in business by going into debt, taking two years off work, and spending the majority of the time learning about how big corporations work from professors who have never owned a business
- Spend endless time sifting through low quality, and non-authoritative free online content from "gurus" with no credentials. Sure, there are countless online articles and eBooks on how to build and grow a business, but every business is unique and generic advice is hardly a suitable substitute for personalized guidance
- Attend numerous conferences hoping to meet a few valuable people or learn a couple of nuggets
- Engage a business coach and mentor

Business Consultants

Business consultants seem to be everywhere. Many consultants have held low-level management positions at large corporations until they were laid off. After a year of searching for a job, they decided to become a consultant in order to start earning money. They are good people; they mean well, but they lack the right experience to coach a small business owner. About 90% of the business consultants I have met have never owned a successful business which I believe is a basic requirement if you are going to help another business owner to grow her business.

Some of these coaches and consultants buy into a licensing agreement or franchise and take an online course that provides them with a framework to help business owners. Unfortunately, the framework is focused on mindsets, motivation, and emotions, and most of the coaching is to motivate the business owner and discussing how he or she feels. Many business coaching programs have essentially become quasi-psychologists for entrepreneurs in search of somebody who will finally understand them and the inherent loneliness often associated with the founding and growing a successful company. Although there is value in hiring therapists, psychologists and life coaches, that is not what business coaching is about.

Good business coaches have been experienced entrepreneurs and business owners themselves who decide to use their talents for building and growing a business to help other business owners reach their goals. Business coaching, when done well, helps business owners grow their businesses as a result of discovering breakthroughs and implementing proven best-practice strategies, plans, systems, and processes, many of which are complex and difficult to implement without proper coaching and mentorship.

If you want to learn how to play an instrument, it's much easier to learn from a teacher than it is to teach yourself. Likewise, if an athlete wants to improve his or her skills, the best thing they can do is join a team that has a great coach. Great coaches and mentors are the quickest routes to success in almost every pursuit, yet the same logic is often overlooked when it comes to growing a business. Having a business coach is much like having a highly experienced partner on your team, and the value that they offer to business owners is priceless. Whether your business is struggling and you need a way to revive it or you simply want to take your brand to the next level, bringing on a professional business coach is one of the most effective options you have available.

Famous Entrepreneurs Who Had Business Coaches

You may be surprised to learn that even some of the world's most famous and successful business owners and entrepreneurs have relied on business coaches at some point in their careers to help them meet their goals.

Eric Schmidt, the former chairman of Google said that "hiring a business coach was the best professional decision he ever made." He admits that it took some urging at first, as he was already a successful CEO of a rapidly growing company. Schmidt wondered, "How could a coach advise me if I'm the best person in the world at this? After being convinced by a Google board member, Schmidt decided to work with a business coach and was amazed by the results. In an interview with Fortune Magazine, Schmidt said, "everyone needs a coach".

Other famous executives and entrepreneurs who have benefited from business coaching include Bill Gates, Steve Jobs, Intuit CEO Steve Bennett, Oprah Winfrey, Bill Clinton, and even Barack Obama have all reported using coaches on a regular basis to advance in their careers. Suffice it to say that business coaching is a resource that some of the world's most successful business owners still swear by to this day.

A Few Head-Turning Business Coaching Statistics

- A study by Manchester Inc. showed that businesses that employed a business coach saw an average return on their investment of 5.7 times the amount that they paid for the coaching services

- A study conducted by Metrix Global LLC showed that businesses that paid for coaching saw a return on their investment of 7.9 times the amount that they paid for the coaching services
- A report conducted by the Personnel Management Association showed that executives who received both coaching and training were able to increase their productivity by 86% compared to a 22% increase in productivity by executives who received training alone
- A Hay Group study showed that 40% of Fortune 500 companies make use of business coaching to train and develop their executives
- 53% of business owners and executives report that it increased their productivity
- 61% of owners report that it increased their job satisfaction
- 23% of executives report that business coaching helped them reduce operational costs
- 22% of companies report that business coaching increased their profitability
- 67% of business owners and executives report that business coaching increased their teamwork skills within their business

These statistics shine a spotlight on the real-world value that business coaching offers. Like anything else your business spends money on, coaching services are an investment, one that surveys and studies show time and time again to deliver significant returns in a variety of key areas. Here are a few more reasons to consider working with a business coach.

What Do Growth Zone University Business Coaches Do?

Growth Zone University business coaches serve as both trainers and mentors, training you in the skills you need to be successful in your business and serving as a source of information should you have questions about what action you should take, and how to affect it. Growth Zone University business coaches work to refine your talents, bring clarity to your goals, guide your decisions, and do everything they can do to ensure that you and your business are successful.

Our Process

Growth Zone University coaches follow a flexible process to ensure that your business and personal goals are achieved. We do this by ensuring that:

- Both business and personal vision statements are articulated
- Your goals are defined with great clarity and your business goals harmonize with your personal goals

Once we know where you want to take your business we can identify what roadblocks you are grappling with that are slowing your growth. We will help you create:

- A strategic business assessment including Financial, Operations, Marketing, Sales, and Administrative functions
- We will work with you to develop a roadmap to achieve your goals
- We will identify areas of strength and weakness of your overall business including those associated with your people, your processes, and your products
- We will map your current information flow and product flow
- We help you identify opportunities as well as potential risks
- We help you explore ways to mitigate potential risks
- We work with you to ensure you achieve your goals

Reasons Business Owners Need Coaches

Every business owner needs help to ensure their business grows enduring value. If you have a great eye for talent, great leadership skills and you can afford to invest in people you can build a team with the experience and expertise you need inside your business. If you have not yet reached that point, you can hire a coach who will teach you while you gain experience in new areas. The tipping point that pushes an owner to decide to hire a coach varies, but the more prevalent situations can be grouped into four categories:

- You don't know what to do
- You are not getting the results you want
- You know what to do but have difficulty implementing
- You want to develop your own capability as a leader

You Don't Know What to Do

Your business has been doing well, but now you have hit a plateau, and you're not sure how to get it going again. Perhaps you're at a crossroads and don't know which path to choose. Should you offer additional products or services? Increase prices? Go after new markets? A business coach who has broad experience in growing businesses is unbiased when it comes to your business, can see a clear path to your growth, and can advise you on steps to take to get there.

You are overwhelmed

Have you reached a point where you feel there is very little time in the day to satisfactorily complete all the tasks on your To-Do list or feel that your revenue stream isn't as strong as it should be, or you feel that you are losing control of your employees, your suppliers, or your business? As you grow your business, everything gets more complex. When you are overwhelmed you will focus on solving the myriad of immediate problems. You don't have the time to focus on strategic issues. As a result, the problems are never resolved, they always come back in another form on another day. That's because you are not solving the problem, you are only treating the symptoms.

Visible problems are usually symptoms of bigger issues that can only be identified through a careful, thorough assessment. Don't waste your time treating symptoms that will come back if the root cause is not identified and addressed. A business coach will take a holistic view of your business, find the underlying cause of the problem and then coach you on how to fix it. Feeling overwhelmed is one of the first signs that you need a business coach.

You're in a Complacency Trap

Have you been feeling indecisive about growing your business? Making a significant change to your business can be a scary daunting decision that is difficult to make. So, you do the easiest thing you can do, nothing. You must remember that what got you to where you are now, will not get you to the next place you want to go. In fact, it won't even keep you where you are. You need to change and that can be scary but a good coach will help you put together a plan that addresses your key concerns and gives you your best chance of success. With the help of an experienced business coach, you will gain a new perspective and confidence in planning and executing strategies. Surveys have shown that among small business owners who have hired a business coach, 70% have seen increased work performance, 86% have seen a significant return on investment and an impressive 99% of owners were happy that they made the decision to hire a business coach. Everyone needs collaboration and advice to conquer the world.

You are not committed to growth

You want to grow your business but you are concerned that spending the money on a coach might not be a good investment. When you make a commitment to engage a growth coach, you are making a commitment to building enduring value. Working with a business coach is a commitment of time and money to achieve returns of 5 to 10 times your investment. When you make a commitment to another person, you are far more likely to follow through and achieve the results you desire.

You are not Getting the Results you Want

You thought you had it all figured out; you put together a plan, but you are not getting the results you wanted. It's not uncommon for business owners to feel that they are on the right path, but find that success eludes them.

Turn your goals into reality

Business coaches have one goal, to turn your goals into reality. From defining your vision, setting your goals, defining your strategy, creating plans, and monitoring progress we work with you every step of the way. If your vision is not clear your goals will not be clear. If your goals are not clear, your strategy will not be as sharp as it should be. If your strategy is weak your plans will be unfocused. If your plans are not crisp, you will never achieve your vision.

We will take you through a proven process that will start with your vision and will not end until you achieve your goals.

Roadblocks

We all encounter roadblocks in business. They're inevitable. Roadblocks can be debilitating if you don't know how to remove them or get around them. A business coach is like having a bulldozer that comes in and removes roadblocks. Coaches have the skills and experience to solve the problems you're facing because they have faced those problems in their own business.

In order to get results you want, you need guidance from someone who can see things from a more objective view. The advice and guidance a coach provides can help you eliminate the roadblocks that are preventing you from achieving your goals. Turning to a business coach can increase ROI, increase employee engagement, and allow you to remove obstacles that are preventing growth.

You have no accountability

You are the boss. You don't answer to anyone. Perhaps that's why you started your business in the beginning. To be free from anyone telling you what to do, or how to do it. To be able to make your own decisions and reap the benefits of owning your own business.

A business coach is your partner, someone to hold you accountable for what you promise yourself. You will be assigned homework. You will have regular check-ins where you discuss progress towards your goals. Your coach will always be there for you ensuring that you're staying the course, gaining the knowledge you need, and growing yourself, and your business.

You have blind spots

Sometimes, when you are too close to something, you can develop blind spots. A good business coach will have an objective point of view, and the ability to quickly identify problem areas that you may not see. They may also offer solutions or strategies you might not have considered, or push you out of your comfort zone so you can take your business to the next level.

Saves time, money and effort

You can learn by experimenting, trying a variety of alternatives, and then picking the alternative that gives you the best results. This process is time-consuming, expensive, and may not result in the optimum solution. Or, you can learn from a coach's experience and get on the fast track to success. It will save you time, money and effort.

Coaching is expensive and I need to save money

One thing that I see often among "do it myself" types is that they read a lot of vague free articles on the internet and haphazardly try everything. Then wonder why they don't get results. They're not getting results because they have no systematic process.

By learning how to build a business on your own you can save pennies while losing dollars due to inefficiencies, money lost on mistaken approaches, and lost opportunities. You can keep experimenting or you can consult a business coach.

Running a healthy, well-managed business leads to both cost savings and growing profits. You will learn how to identify inefficiencies in your company and learning how to fix them, so you can save more in the long-term. Not fixing these problems means profit is leaking from your business every day.

You are not implementing

You've made plans to develop new products, but they never come to fruition. You know you need an inventory control system, but you can't seem to choose which one. You know you don't have the staff you need to really grow the way you want, but you don't want to rock the boat.

Oftentimes, even the best of us exhibit behaviors that are less than helpful. We avoid making hard decisions or lie to ourselves from time to time. As a result, you break the promises you made to yourself. And you can't get out of the traps you've fallen into.

You need a coach when you know what to do but don't implement the actions. You need someone to help you translate general principles into specific steps that you can take in your own business. Being held accountable increases the chances of getting anything done. And a business coach is a great way to leverage accountability.

Doing it alone is hard

You're proud of how you've started and grown your business on your own, but consider how much easier it would be (and how much faster you could grow it) if you had help. Hiring a business coach isn't admitting failure. Not by a long shot. In fact, it's one of the smartest things you can do because it says you're dedicated to helping your business thrive, and you know that you can do that faster with help. Hiring the right professionals (whether that's a writer, an accountant or a coach) indicates that you're serious about success and won't let your own ego stand in the way. If you're serious about growing your business this year, hire a business coach.

You have no confidante or mentor

Your employees look up to you. They expect only excellence from you, and they can be intimidated and may not always be honest with you, especially if you ask them for feedback on one of your ideas.

You may be embarrassed to tell them that you don't how to handle the current situation. You may be afraid to ask for their help, because you think you should be giving them advice, not soliciting it from them. You reason that you are the boss, and you are supposed to have all the answers.

If you want to discuss things without feeling vulnerable or exposed and want your reputation and credibility to remain intact, you should speak with a business coach. This person can be your sounding board and will provide you honest feedback about all your ideas and plans.

Experience

Your experience is limited to what you know from running your own business, as well as any jobs you held before you were an entrepreneur. An experienced business coach has "been there and done that" with their own business and also has the wisdom that comes from years of working with many types of companies and business owners from all walks of life. She will share what she's learned from working with other businesses and challenge your thinking, goals, and willingness to grow.

Motivate you to think bigger and take your business to the next level

There are times when you are aware of what has to be done, but can't find the drive to actually do it. You have some fuzzy ideas about how to grow, but you don't know how to implement those ideas.

Even if you're ambitious and driven, sometimes you need another person to give you a push to think beyond your limits. A business coach asks questions that challenge you to think critically about your business and provides encouragement when you need it most. He will nudge you out of your comfort zone and back into the growth zone, where you and your business can flourish. You'll be able to achieve more than you ever thought possible!

You want a sounding board for ideas

It can be isolating when you're a management team of one. No one is around to tell you if something is a bad idea. Nobody challenges you. No one realigns you in a better direction when you get off course.

Two heads are better than one, especially if one head belongs to a coach with experience and expertise. A coach will challenge you to grow your business to its fullest potential. Challenges, obstacles, roadblocks, plateaus, blind spots – they have seen it all. They have even experienced it themselves, and that is why you need a business coach to be your sounding board. A coach works with you in a spirit of informed collaboration so that you make smart business decisions and receive powerful guidance to build enduring value. For business owners at every level, continued growth can be elusive. A business coach is equipped to not only know the way but lead the way for you. Let them do it! It's what they do best.

Personal Development

Growth involves change. Think of coaching as a learning experience. The goal is to transfer knowledge and know-how to you and your management team. Business coaching is about teaching you how to fish, not fishing for you. It's about teaching you the knowledge and skills to address problems on your own. You will be pushed to step outside your comfort zone, meet new people and try new things.

Target and Identify Strengths

Tapping into your strengths can help you achieve your true potential. Unfortunately, many of us tend to get in our own way. We become unable to recognize what we do best. A coach can help you pinpoint your strengths and suggest ways to build on them.

Building Confidence

Confidence in business is invaluable. It is the result of having knowledge, experience, and preparation. Being supported by a great coach and giving yourself the space to work out challenges enhances your confidence when going into major situations, dealing with crises, or handling conflict. A professional sounding board keeps you sharp and playing your best game.

Combating Unconscious Incompetence

There are things we don't know we don't know. A coach provides another set of eyes that can draw on experiences with other clients in order to reveal and mitigate blind spots in your business.

Building Connections

So much of success is based on the connections you have. As the saying goes, "Your network is your net worth." Then there's also the piece of wisdom about being the average of the 5 people you spend the most time around. It's not what you know, but who you know and what they are willing to do for you. If you want a really successful business, then you need to have a great source of relevant connections in your network that you can call on when you need them. If you build a good relationship with a business coach, they become a connection for life.

And through them, you'll meet other successful people and it becomes a snowball effect. The more you are involved with successful people, the more you will succeed. Networking opportunities skyrocket when your business coach is out being an advocate for you.

Smarter financial planning

Running the numbers for many owners is often one of the most challenging parts of running their business. Your business coach will help you with everything from understanding financial reports to developing a budget to pricing new services. You can come to her with any financial question and be confident that you're making a smart decision for your business.

Your Story

Your story is not fully written, or it might appear here. That story could be a shining example of a business that grew to $50M in revenue, or it could be the story of a business owner who fell into a complacency trap and never found her way out. Whichever way the story turns, you will write that story. But you do not need to write it alone. I would be honored to play a small part in helping your story to be one of success.

Key Takeaways

I have outlined the top 10 roadblocks to growing a successful business. You may have already encountered several of these road-blocks, and you may be grappling with some right now. If you can't seem to break through one of these, if your revenue has plateaued and you don't know what to do, get help. You don't need to call us, but you should call someone who can help you.

If this book resonates with you and you can relate to the road-blocks discussed in the chapters you've read, then contact my office for a Complimentary Growth Strategy Consultation (value $995.00) or visit https://BRGBrokers.com/FreeConsult

Best wishes to your continued Growth!

Lightning Source UK Ltd.
Milton Keynes UK
UKHW040907281119
354396UK00010B/1344/P